Progressive Problems for 'S' Grade Physics

by

W. Kennedy

Hodder Gibson

A MEMBER OF THE HODDER HEADLINE GROUP

PREFACE

Progressive Problems for Standard Grade Physics covers the topics studied for the SQA Standard Grade Physics syllabus. It contains **a planned sequence of questions** constructed to guide the pupil systematically from the simplest to the most difficult problems thereby laying a firm foundation to build upon.

This method of problem solving helps to overcome the difficulties associated with mixed ability classes by encouraging the slow learner while stretching the more able pupils.

In addition to the progressive nature of the problems, the book has been subject-categorised to give a breakdown of every aspect of the course. [This enables the teacher to pick his own area and, where appropriate, alter the order of teaching to suit individual needs.]

The material has been used extensively. It has been closely monitored as to its value and relevance to the learning process. Consequently it has been developed and refined to its present level.

W. Kennedy, 1999.

ACKNOWLEDGEMENTS

I would like to thank the physics department, staff and pupils of St. Mungo's High School, Falkirk, who trialled the materials and helped to refine them.

Orders: please contact Bookpoint Ltd, 130 Milton Park, Abingdon, Oxon OX14 4SB. Telephone: (44) 01235 827720. Fax: (44) 01235 400454. Lines are open from 9.00–5.00, Monday to Saturday, with a 24 hour message answering service. You can also order through our website www.hoddereducation.co.uk.

Papers used in this book are natural, renewable and recyclable products. They are made from wood grown in sustainable forests. The logging and manufacturing processes conform to the environmental regulations of the country of origin.

British Library Cataloguing in Publication Data
A catalogue record for this title is available from the British Library

ISBN-13: 978-0-716-93233-8

Published by Hodder Gibson, 2a Christie Street, Paisley PA1 1NB.
Tel: 0141 848 1609; Fax: 0141 889 6315; Email: hoddergibson@hodder.co.uk
First Published 1999
Impression number   11 10 9 8 7 6 5 4 3
Year   2010 2009 2008 2007

Copyright © 1999 W Kennedy

Printed in Great Britain for Hodder Gibson, 2a Christie Street, Paisley, PA1 1NB, Scotland, UK

CONTENTS

DATA SHEET

Speed of light in materials

Material	Speed in m/s
Air	3.0×10^8
Carbon dioxide	3.0×10^8
Diamond	1.2×10^8
Glass	2.0×10^8
Glycerol	2.1×10^8
Water	2.3×10^8

Speed of sound in materials

Material	Speed in m/s
Aluminium	5200
Air	340
Bone	4100
Carbon dioxide	270
Glycerol	1900
Muscle	1600
Steel	5200
Tissue	1500
Water	1500

Gravitational field strengths

	Gravitational field strength on the surface in N/kg
Earth	10
Jupiter	26
Mars	4
Mercury	4
Moon	1.6
Neptune	12
Saturn	11
Sun	270
Venus	9

Specific heat capacity of materials

Material	Specific heat capacity in J/kg °C
Alcohol	2350
Aluminium	902
Copper	386
Glass	500
Glycerol	2400
Ice	2100
Lead	128
Silica	1033
Water	4180

Specific latent heat of fusion of materials

Material	Specific latent heat of fusion in J/kg
Alcohol	0.99×10^5
Aluminium	3.95×10^5
Carbon dioxide	1.80×10^5
Copper	2.05×10^5
Glycerol	1.81×10^5
Lead	0.25×10^5
Water	3.34×10^5

Melting and boiling points of materials

Material	Melting point in °C	Boiling point in °C
Alcohol	−98	65
Aluminium	660	2470
Copper	1077	2567
Glycerol	18	290
Lead	328	1737
Turpentine	−10	156

Specific latent heat of vaporisation of materials

Material	Specific latent heat of vaporisation in J/kg
Alcohol	11.2×10^5
Carbon dioxide	3.77×10^5
Glycerol	8.30×10^5
Turpentine	2.90×10^5
Water	22.6×10^5

SI Prefixes and Multiplication Factors

Prefix	Symbol	Factor	
giga	G	1 000 000 000	$= 10^9$
mega	M	1 000 000	$= 10^6$
kilo	k	1000	$= 10^3$
milli	m	0.001	$= 10^{-3}$
micro	μ	0.000 001	$= 10^{-6}$
nano	n	0.000 000 001	$= 10^{-9}$

FORMULAE LIST

Telecommunications

$$d = vt$$
$$c = f\lambda$$
$$f = \frac{1}{T}$$

Electricity

$$Q = It$$
$$R_T = R_1 + R_2 + R_3 \quad \text{(series)}$$
$$\frac{1}{R_T} = \frac{1}{R_1} + \frac{1}{R_2} + \frac{1}{R_3} \quad \text{(parallel)}$$
$$V = IR$$
$$V_1 = \frac{R_1}{R_T} \times V_{supply} \quad \text{(voltage division)}$$
$$P = \frac{E}{t}$$
$$P = VI = I^2R = \frac{V^2}{R}$$

Health Physics

$$P = \frac{1}{f}$$

Electronics

$$\text{Voltage gain} = \frac{\text{output voltage}}{\text{input voltage}}$$
$$\text{Power gain} = \frac{\text{output power}}{\text{input power}}$$

Transport

$$a = \frac{v-u}{t}$$
$$W = mg$$
$$F = ma$$
$$W.D. = Fd$$
$$E_p = mgh$$
$$E_k = \frac{1}{2}mv^2$$

Energy Matters

$$\text{Efficiency} = \frac{\text{energy out}}{\text{energy in}} \times 100\%$$
$$\frac{V_p}{V_s} = \frac{N_p}{N_s}$$
Power in = Power out $\quad$ (assuming transformer is 100% efficient)
$$E_h = cm\Delta T \quad \text{(specific heat capacity)}$$
$$E_h = mL \quad \text{(latent heat)}$$

Space

$$mv \qquad = \qquad mv$$
(to the left) $\qquad$ (to the right)

UNIT 1

TELECOMMUNICATIONS

SECTION 1

SPEED OF SOUND

1. At a cricket match, a spectator in the crowd sees a batsman hit a ball. After a short delay the spectator hears the sound of the impact. Why is there a delay?

2. The apparatus shown is used to measure the speed of sound.

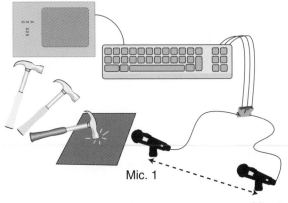

   (a) Explain how it works.

   (b) What two measurements are taken from this apparatus?

3. At 1 o'clock a gun is fired from Edinburgh Castle.

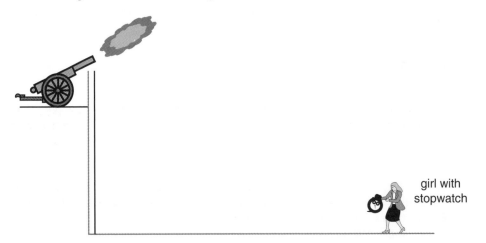

   A girl is trying to measure the speed of sound. She sees the puff of smoke when the gun is fired and then after a short delay she hears the "bang".

   (a) When does she start the stopwatch?

   (b) When does she stop the stopwatch?

   (c) What other measurement does she need in order to calculate the speed of sound?

4. The girl in question 3 obtains the following results.

   Time on stopwatch = 2·5 s.

   Distance between girl and castle = 850 m.

What result will these measurements give for the speed of sound?

5. The speed of sound in air is 340 m/s. How far will sound travel in

   (a) 2 seconds,

   (b) 7 seconds?

6. The speed of sound in air is 340 m/s. How long does it take sound to travel

   (a) 1700 m,

   (b) 1020 m?

7. The speed of sound in water is 1500 m/s. How far will sound travel (in water) in

   (a) 20 seconds,

   (b) 1 minute?

8. The speed of sound in water is 1500 m/s. How long does it take sound (in water) to travel

   (a) 15 km,

   (b) 300 m?

9. You are standing on a straight road when you see a flash of lightning in the sky ahead. Four seconds later you hear a peal of thunder. How far would you have to walk before coming to a tree that had been struck by the lightning? The speed of sound is 340 m/s.

10. Two boys, A and B, standing together shout to a friend C who is exactly 340 m away. Boy A's sound wave has a frequency of 200 Hz and boy B's wave has a frequency of 250 Hz. If the speed of sound is 340 m/s, which boy does C hear first?

11. A boy shouts up a canyon and 3 s later hears the echo of the sound wave.

   If the velocity of sound in air is 340 m/s, how far is he from the canyon wall?

12. A sonic depth finder on a ship sends out a pulse of sound and detects the reflected pulse 0·2 seconds later. If the velocity of sound in water is 1500 m/s, how deep is the sea bed?

WAVES

1. Draw three full waves and mark on your diagram:

   (a) the wavelength;

   (b) the amplitude.

2. A sound wave activates a microphone connected to a cathode ray oscilloscope. The trace obtained is shown in X. With the oscilloscope controls unaltered, the sound is changed and the new trace is shown in Y.

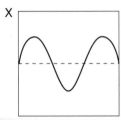
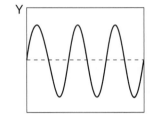

   (a) Which wave has the bigger amplitude?

   (b) Which wave has the bigger frequency?

3. Study the wave diagram below.

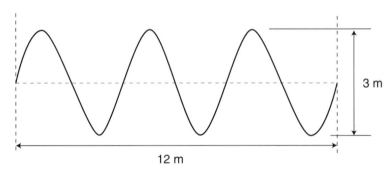

3 m

12 m

   (a) What is the wavelength?

   (b) What is the amplitude?

4. A vibrator in a ripple tank produces 10 waves per second.

   (a) What is the frequency of the waves?

   (b) How many waves are produced in one minute?

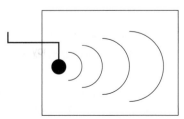

5.   A water wave travels 15 cm in 3 s.

     Calculate the velocity of the wave.

6.   The plan view of a ripple tank shows the wave crests represented as lines in the diagram
     below.

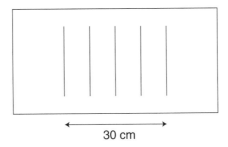

                                30 cm

(a) How many wave crests are shown?

(b) How big is each wavelength?

(c) If the frequency of the vibrator is 6 Hz, calculate the velocity of the waves.

THE WAVE EQUATION

1.   A pupil counts 20 waves passing a point in 10 s. What is the frequency of the waves?

2.   If the frequency of waves in a ripple tank is 10 Hz and the wavelength is 4 cm, what is the
     velocity of the waves?

3.   If the frequency of waves in a ripple tank is 5 Hz and the wavelength is 7 cm, what is the
     velocity of the waves?

4.   The velocity of sound is 340 m/s. If the frequency of a sound wave is 80 Hz, find the
     wavelength.

5.   Find the wavelength of a water wave of frequency 40 Hz travelling at 120 cm/s.

6.   If the velocity of waves in a ripple tank is 0·6 m/s and the wavelength of each wave is
     5 cm, what is the frequency of the disturbance?

7.   What is the frequency of a strobe lamp which "stops" a water wave of wavelength 2·5 cm
     travelling at 0·5 m/s? Assume this is the greatest frequency of the strobe which does not
     give double viewing.

8. Calculate the unknown (v, λ or f) in the table below.

	v	λ	f
(a)	?	6 cm	50 Hz
(b)	1·44 m/s	?	24 Hz
(c)	340 m/s	?	40 Hz
(d)	3×10^8 m/s	300 m	?
(e)	3×10^8 m/s	?	1×10^{10} Hz
(f)	1500 m/s	75 cm	?

9. If sound waves travel at 1500 m/s in water, what is the wavelength of a 30 Hz note in water?

10. A water wave of wavelength 3 cm travels 20 cm in 5 s.

    (a) What is the velocity of the wave?

    (b) What is the frequency of the wave?

11. A wave of wavelength 5 cm travels 120 cm in 1 minute.

    (a) What is the velocity of the wave?

    (b) What is the frequency of the wave?

12. A sound wave generator produces 25 waves every 0·1 s. If the velocity of sound is 340 m/s, what is the wavelength of the wave produced?

13. A wave takes 0·75 s to travel 3 m. The generator making the wave vibrates 120 times per minute. Find the wavelength of the wave.

14. One water wave (A) has a wavelength of 6 cm and a frequency of 50 Hz. Another water wave (B) travels 250 m in 1 min 40 s. Which wave travels faster — and by how much?

15. Water waves travel from one side of a pond to the other, a distance of 18 m, in 4·5 s. The distance between two successive wave crests is 8 cm. What is the frequency of the waves?

SECTION 2

COMMUNICATION THROUGH CABLES

1. Copy the diagram of the morse code system.

(a) Mark in the transmitter and receiver.

(b) How could a word be sent from transmitter to receiver?

2. Could a morse code system be made with a light?

3. The diagram below shows a telephone handset.

(a) Which part is the earpiece?

(b) Is the earpiece a transmitter or a receiver?

(c) Which part is the mouthpiece?

(d) Is the mouthpiece a transmitter or receiver?

4. In the telephone handset in question 3:

(a) What does the mouthpiece contain?

(b) What is the energy change in this piece of electrical equipment?

(c) What does the earpiece contain?

(d) What is the energy change in this piece of electrical equipment?

5.   John uses a demonstration telephone link to speak to Karen.

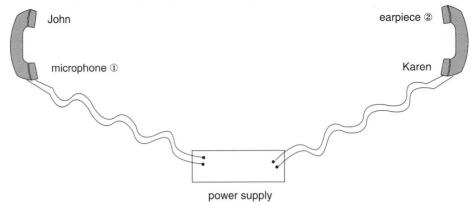

The electrical signal travels through wires to Karen at a speed which is:

A   340 m/s;

B   100 000 m/s;

C 2×10^8 m/s;

D   almost 3×10^8 m/s?

6.   A microphone detects sounds and displays them on an oscilloscope screen. The oscilloscope controls are **not altered** as the microphone is used to pick up sound P and then sound Q.

P   Q

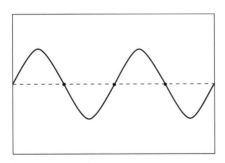   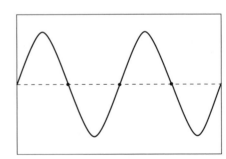

(a)   What do both sounds have in common?

(b)   What is the difference between sound P and sound Q?

7. A microphone detects sounds and displays them on an oscilloscope screen. The oscilloscope controls are **not altered** as the microphone is used to pick up sound R and then sound S.

R 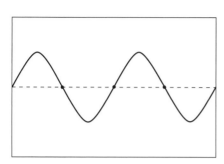   S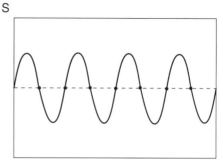

(a) What do both sounds have in common?

(b) What is the difference between sound R and sound S?

8. Pitch is another word for frequency.

True or false?

REFLECTION

1. Copy and complete the following diagrams showing what happens to the light after reflection.

(a)   *(b)*   *(c)*

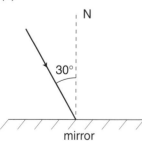   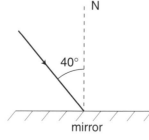   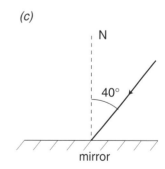

2.   A home-made periscope uses two parallel mirrors (M_1 and M_2).

Copy and complete the diagram showing how light entering the periscope reaches the observer's eye.

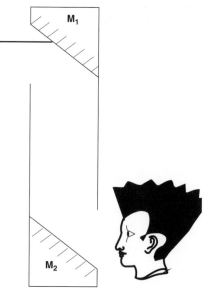

3.   Copy and complete the following diagrams showing what happens to the light after reflection.

(a)

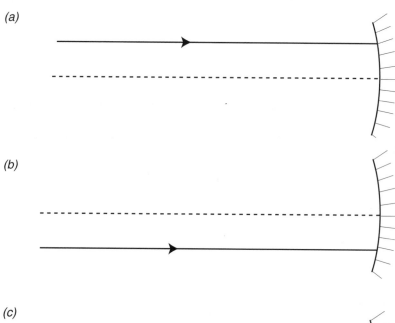

(b)

(c)

4. A bulb is placed at X at the focal point of a curved reflector in order to produce a parallel beam of light in the laboratory.

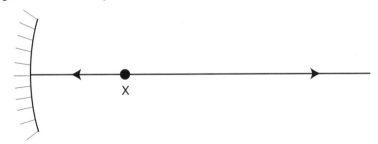

Copy the diagram and draw in the missing rays.

5. A famous demonstration of the effect shown in question 4 uses a strong electrical heater at the focal point (X) of a highly polished metal reflector.

An unlit match is placed at Y, at the focal point of a second highly polished metal reflector.

(a) Copy the diagram carefully (suggest graph paper) and draw the heat rays coming from X.

(b) Do the heat rays reflect off both metal reflectors?

(c) What happens to the match at Y?

(d) Are the infra-red rays concentrated at Y?

REFRACTION

1. Copy and complete the following diagrams showing what happens to the light in the glass and after it has passed through.

2. Copy and complete the following diagrams showing what happens to the light.

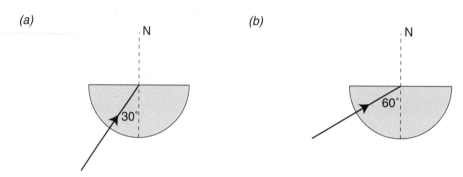

3. (a) The critical angle for glass is 42°. What is meant by critical angle?

    (b) In which diagram in question 2 does total internal reflection occur?

4.   Light travels along an optical fibre by total internal reflection.

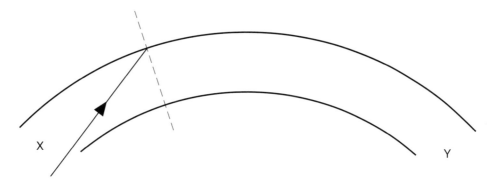

Copy and complete the diagram showing how light travels from X to Y.

5.   A certain type of Christmas tree uses optical fibres. If the lamp is in the base of the tree, how does light reach all parts of the tree?

6.   What are the energy changes in an optical fibre telephone system? You must start and finish with sound.

7.   Light travels at 2×10^8 m/s in glass. How long does it take to travel along an optical fibre which is 10 km long?

8.   Which system requires more repeaters per km of cable — standard copper wire or optical fibre?

SECTION 3

RADIO AND TELEVISION

1. *(a)* Copy and complete the block diagram for the main parts of a radio.

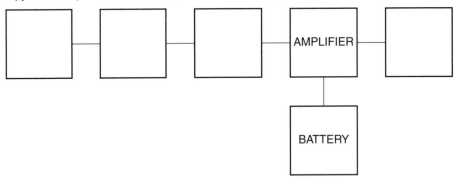

(b) What does the amplifier do to the signal?

(c) From where does the amplifier derive its power?

2. *(a)* What is the purpose of the aerial?

(b) What is the purpose of the tuner?

(c) What is the energy change in the loudspeaker?

3. John has a pocket transistor radio in the playground. It is receiving Radio 1 but the signal is weak and the radio output is quiet.

When John puts the radio against a metal down pipe from the school gutters, the radio immediately gets much louder.

Explain.

4. In the laboratory, a simple experiment with a file, a battery and a radio demonstrates interference.

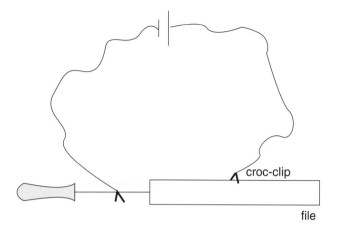

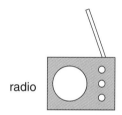

(a) If the croc-clip is stationary, describe the radio reception.

(b) Scraping the croc-clip across the file alters the radio reception. How?

(c) Explain what is happening using the word "interference".

5. (a) Ann is in her dad's car listening to the radio on the way to town.

   When the car passes under a bridge, the radio goes very quiet and "crackles".

   What is happening to the signal?

(b) On the way back from town, Ann is listening to a tape playing in the car.

   When the car passes under the same bridge there is no change in the volume or quality of the sound Ann is listening to.

   Why not?

6. A laboratory demonstration shows a signal before and after it has passed through a decoder.

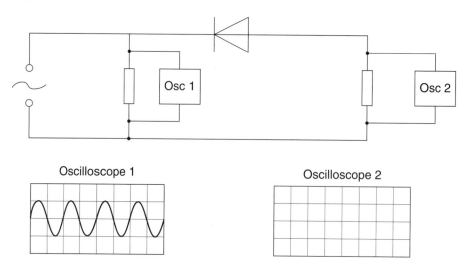

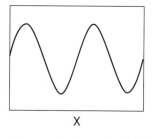

Oscilloscope 1

Oscilloscope 2

(a) Which oscilloscope shows the picture before the decoder?

(b) Copy and complete the diagram for oscilloscope 2 (use graph paper).

7. Clare was trying to explain modulation in simple terms to her young brother.

She said "You know Radio 1 and the DJ in London ... well it's a bit like a lorry that leaves London with a load of food for Glasgow. The radio wave is like the lorry ..."

Complete Clare's analogy.

8. Look at the three waveforms below.

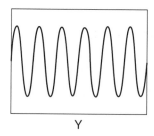

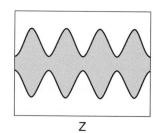

X   Y   Z

(a) Which signal is the audio wave?

(b) Which signal is the radio wave?

(c) Which signal is the modulated wave?

(d) Make an equation linking X, Y and Z.

9. Copy and complete the block diagam for the main parts of a television.

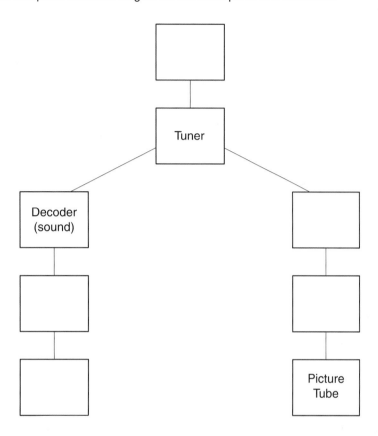

10. Referring back to question 9:

   (a) What is the purpose of the tuner?

   (b) What is the energy charge in the picture tube?

11. An electron gun inside a television is shown below.

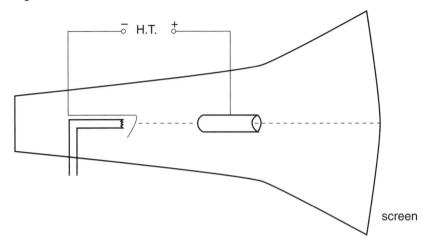

Copy the diagram and label

       anode   cathode   heater.

12. *(a)* What would an observer watching the screen in question 11 see?

    (b) When an electron strikes the screen, what is the energy change?

13. An electron gun inside an oscilloscope is shown below.

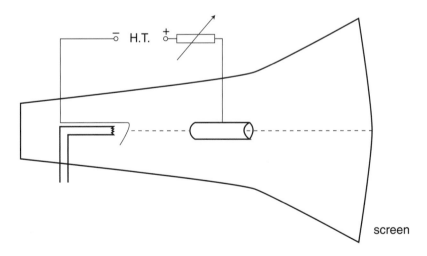

(a) Are electrons attracted by the anode?

(b) Why do the electrons not stop at the anode?

(c) The rheostat can vary the anode voltage. It's actually the brightness control on the oscilloscope.

    How does it make the spot brighter?

14. How many lines are there in one TV picture?

15. How many pictures are produced in one second?

16. What is the time between one picture and the next?

17. What is image retention?

18. *(a)* How does a cartoon figure move smoothly?

   (b) How does a TV picture move smoothly to the next picture?

19. How many electron guns are there in a black and white TV set?

20. How many electron guns are there in a colour TV set?

21. What are the three primary colours in a colour TV set?

22. Copy and complete the four lines below showing what colours are formed when the primary colours are mixed inside a colour television.

   red   +   green   =

   red   +   blue   =

   green   +   blue   =

   red   +   green   +   blue   =

SECTION 4

TRANSMISSION OF RADIO WAVES

1. Microwave, radio and TV signals all travel (in air) at

    A   340 m/s,

    B   1500 m/s,

    C 2×10^8 m/s,

    D 3×10^8 m/s?

2. How long does it take

    (a) light to travel 600 km through air,

    (b) a radio signal to travel 900 km through air?

3. How long does it take light to travel 40 km through an optical fibre? (Speed of light in glass is 2×10^8 m/s.)

4. (a) Radio Clyde used to broadcast at 261 m on the medium wave (MW) band. Calculate the frequency of the transmission.

    (b) Radio Clyde now broadcasts at 102·5 MHz (FM). Calculate the wavelength of the transmission.

    (c) What does FM stand for?

5. A satellite receives signals at a frequency of 5 GHz (1 GHz = 1×10^9 Hz).

    Calculate the wavelength of the signal.

DIFFRACTION

1. Copy and complete the diagrams below showing how plane water waves diffract.

    (a)

    (b)

    (c)
    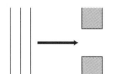

    (d)
    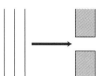

2. Copy and complete the diagrams below showing how plane water waves diffract.

    (a)

    (b)
    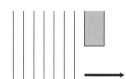

    (c) By making reference to parts *(a)* and *(b),* finish the conclusion:

    The longer the wavelength (   ), the .... the diffraction.

3. A transmitter sends out both TV and radio waves in all directions. A range of hills lies between the transmitter and a house.

    The house, well within the transmitting range for TV waves and radio waves, can pick up the radio waves but **not** the TV waves.

    (a) Do radio waves diffract?

    (b) Do TV waves diffract?

    (c) How do the radio waves reach the house?

    (d) Why do the TV waves not reach the house?

4. The man in the house in question 3 decides to buy a satellite dish.

    (a) Will he receive TV waves now?

    (b) Why?

    (c) Will he still receive radio waves?

    (d) Why?

5. Marconi was the first person to send a radio transmission from Britain to America.

    (a) The earth is curved. There were no satellites at that time. How did the waves reach America?

    (b) Did Marconi use long or short wavelengths?

SATELLITES

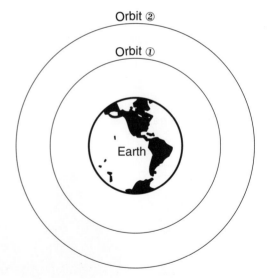

Orbit ②

Orbit ①

Earth

1. Copy and complete.

    (a) The higher the orbit of a satellite, the .... the period.

    (b) Orbit ① is close to the earth so the period is long / short.

    (c) Orbit ② is further away so the period is long / short.

2. *(a)* What is a geostationary satellite?

    (b) What is the period of a geostationary satellite?

    (c) The height of a geostationary satellite is 36 000 km above the earth. True or false?

3. Study the diagram.

    (a) Explain how the dish aerial at the ground station sends signals to the satellite.

    (b) How does the satellite receive these signals?

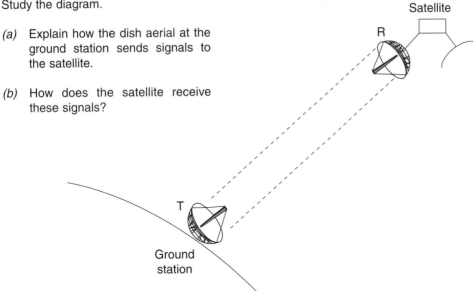

4. Britain sends TV signals to America.

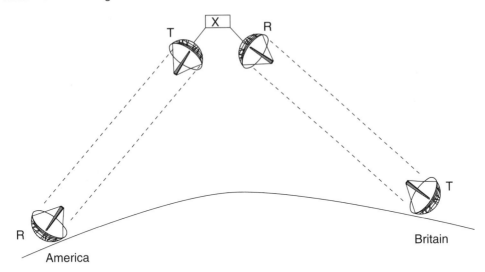

    (a) Making reference to the diagram above, explain the sequence of transmission and reception.

    (b) We often talk about "bouncing" a signal off a satellite. Why is this not true?

    (c) What is inside the satellite at X?

5. Look back to the diagram in question 4. The satellite receives signals, amplifies them and then transmits the signals on to America.

(a) Why is the amplifier necessary?

(b) Comment on the **frequency of the signal received** by the satellite and the **frequency of the signal transmitted** on to America.

FROM THE WALL SOCKET

1. Copy and complete the table below showing the main energy change in each electrical appliance.

Appliance	Main energy change
Bulb	
Cooker	
Hairdryer	
Electric fire	Electrical ⟶ heat
Electric drill	
Vacuum cleaner	
Kettle	

2. Copy and complete the table below showing **approximate** power ratings for these household appliances.

Appliance	Power rating (w)
Electric fire	
Bulb (bedside)	
Electric drill	
TV	
Hairdryer	
Kettle	
Cooker	

3. In the tables above, the cooker is the only appliance you would not "plug in". It has to be wired separately. Why does it not have a plug like all these other appliances?

Data Table for questions 4 and 5

Flex type	Flex current rating (A)	Flex designed for appliances of maximum power (W)
A	13	2990
B	10	2300
C	6	1380
D	3	690

4. From the data table above, choose the correct flex for the following appliances:

  (a) Kettle   2·5 kw

  (b) Lamp   60 w

  (c) TV   250 w

  (d) Heater   2 kw.

5. From the data table above, choose the correct fuse for the following appliances:

  (a) Kettle   2·5 kw

  (b) Lamp   60 w

  (c) TV   250 w

  (d) Heater   2 kw.

6. In the 3-pin plug, name

  (a) Pin X;

  (b) Pin Y;

  (c) Pin Z.

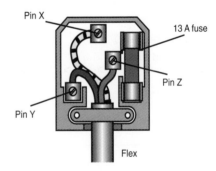

7. When wiring a 3-pin plug, what colour of cable should be connected to:

  (a) X,

  (b) Y,

  (c) Z?

8. *(a)* Is the fuse always connected to the live wire?

  (b) What difference would it make connecting it to the neutral wire?

9. John goes into his bathroom. In order to switch on the bathroom light he has to flick a switch **outside** the bathroom door.

Why is the switch not inside the bathroom?

10. Draw the symbol for double insulation.

11. The double insulation symbol appears on a hairdryer. The flex has only two wires compared with a 3-wire flex.

Which wire is missing?

12. In an electric fire, the earth wire is connected to the metal casing. Imagine there is a fault in the fire and the live wire touches the casing.

    (a) Where does this electricity go?

    (b) What happens to the fuse?

    (c) What would happen if the fire had been wired using a 2-core cable, i.e. no earth connection?

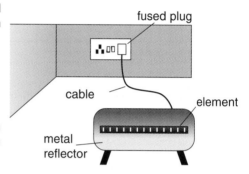

single bar electric fire

13. A vacuum cleaner has a power rating of 650 W. This would mean a 3 A fuse should be connected in the plug.

In fact, a 13 A fuse is required. Explain.

SECTION 2

A.C. AND D.C.

1. Copy and complete the sentence:

    A direct current (d.c.) flows in one direction all the time, but an alternating current (a.c.)

    ....

2. Copy and complete the sentence:

    A battery supplies .... current whereas the mains

    supplies .... current.

3. *(a)* What is the quoted value of the mains voltage?

    (b) Is the peak value of the mains voltage 163 v, 230 v or 325 v?

4. *(a)* What is the frequency of the a.c. current from the mains supply?

    (b) Using the answer to part *(a)*, how many currents are there in 1 second?

5. Draw the symbols for each of the following circuit components.

    bulb   diode

    battery   capacitor

    switch   resistor

    fuse   rheostat

    ammeter   voltmeter

OSCILLOSCOPES AND VOLTAGE

1. Copy and complete the oscilloscope pictures for each of the circuits below.

(a)

CRO

(b)

CRO

2.

3
div

This oscilloscope is set at 5 v / div.

(a) Is the voltage a.c. or d.c.?

(b) Calculate the voltage.

3.

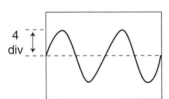

4
div

This oscilloscope is set at 5 v / div.

(a) Is the voltage a.c. or d.c.?

(b) Calculate the peak voltage.

4.

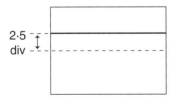

2·5
div

This oscilloscope is set at 3 v / div.

(a) Is the voltage a.c. or d.c.?

(b) Calculate the voltage.

5.

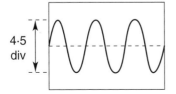

4·5
div

This oscilloscope is set at 3 v / div.

(a) Is the voltage a.c. or d.c.?

(b) Calculate the peak voltage.

OSCILLOSCOPES AND FREQUENCY

1.   An a.c. source of frequency 200 Hz is connected across an oscilloscope and the pattern shown is obtained.

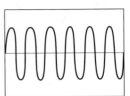

   (a) With the oscilloscope controls unaltered, a signal of frequency 400 Hz is connected to the input. Draw the new pattern obtained.

   (b) Repeat (a) for an input of 100 Hz.

2.

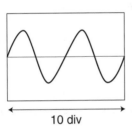

10 div

This oscilloscope time base is set at 10 m s / div.

(a) What is the time for 1 wave on the screen?

(b) Calculate the frequency.

3.

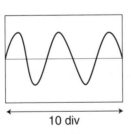

10 div

This oscilloscope time base is set at 1 m s / div.

(a) What is the time for 1 wave on the screen?

(b) Calculate the frequency.

4.

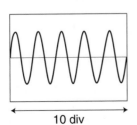

10 div

This oscilloscope time base is set at 10 m s / div.

(a) What is the time for 1 wave on the screen?

(b) Calculate the frequency.

5.

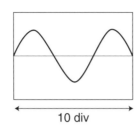

10 div

This oscilloscope time base is set at 100 m s / div.

(a) What is the time for 1 wave on the screen?

(b) Calculate the frequency.

CHARGE — CURRENT — TIME

1.   How much charge flows through a heater in 15 seconds if the current in the heater is 4 A?

2.   A current of 0·5 A flows through a bulb for 5 minutes.

   How much charge has passed through the bulb?

3.   180 C of charge is drawn from a battery every minute.

   (a)   Calculate the current leaving the battery.

   (b)   What is the current returning to the battery?

4.   Calculate the current in a circuit if $7·2 \times 10^3$ C of charge are transferred every hour.

5.   How long will it take to transfer a charge of 26 C through a bulb if the current in the bulb is 2 A?

6.   How long will it take to pass a charge of 1 C through a diode if the maximum current permitted by the diode is 2·5 mA?

7.   The charge on 1 electron is $1·6 \times 10^{-19}$ C.

   How many electrons are required to make a charge of $1·12 \times 10^{-18}$ C?

8.   The charge on 1 electron is $1·6 \times 10^{-19}$ C.

   Explain why it is impossible to make a charge of $1·84 \times 10^{-18}$ C.

SECTIONS 3 AND 4

RESISTORS IN SERIES

Find the total resistance between points x and y in each of the circuits below.

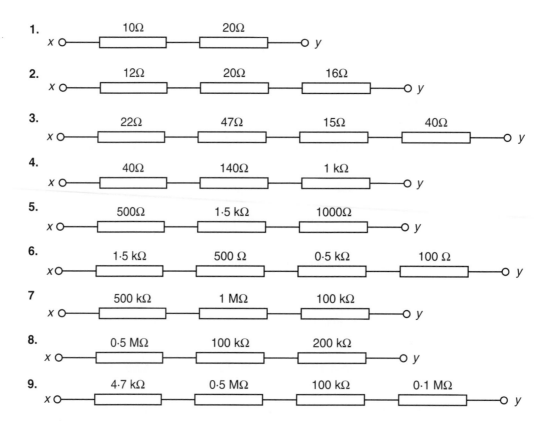

1.   10Ω   20Ω

2.   12Ω   20Ω   16Ω

3.   22Ω   47Ω   15Ω   40Ω

4.   40Ω   140Ω   1 kΩ

5.   500Ω   1·5 kΩ   1000Ω

6.   1·5 kΩ   500 Ω   0·5 kΩ   100 Ω

7   500 kΩ   1 MΩ   100 kΩ

8.   0·5 MΩ   100 kΩ   200 kΩ

9.   4·7 kΩ   0·5 MΩ   100 kΩ   0·1 MΩ

10.   Given the total resistance between x and y is 1000 Ω, find R_X.

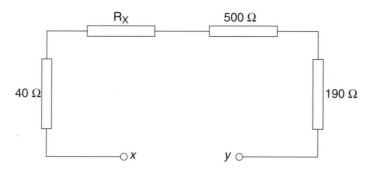

RESISTORS IN PARALLEL

Find the total resistance between points x and y in each of the circuits below.

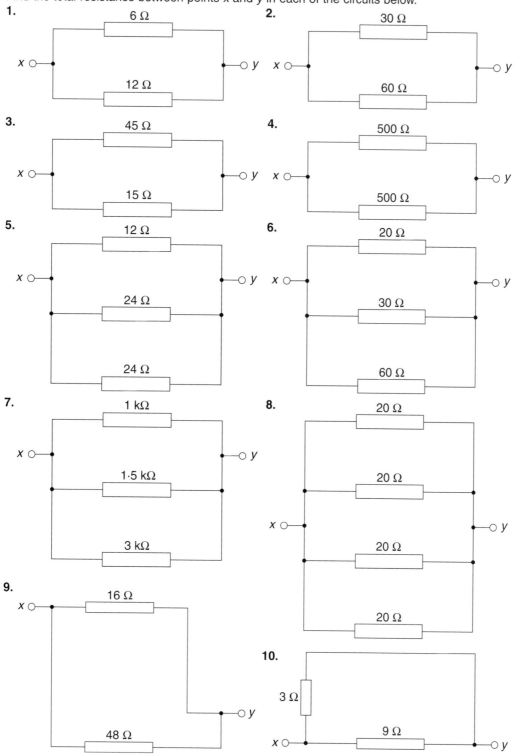

1. 6 Ω 12 Ω

2. 30 Ω 60 Ω

3. 45 Ω 15 Ω

4. 500 Ω 500 Ω

5. 12 Ω 24 Ω 24 Ω

6. 20 Ω 30 Ω 60 Ω

7. 1 kΩ 1·5 kΩ 3 kΩ

8. 20 Ω 20 Ω 20 Ω 20 Ω

9. 16 Ω 48 Ω

10. 3 Ω 9 Ω

COMBINATIONS OF SERIES AND PARALLEL RESISTORS

Find the total resistance between points *x* and *y* in each of the circuits below.

1.

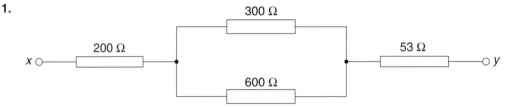

2.

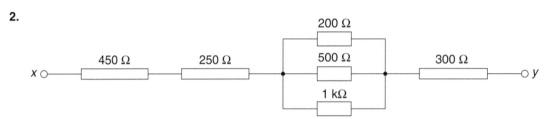

3.

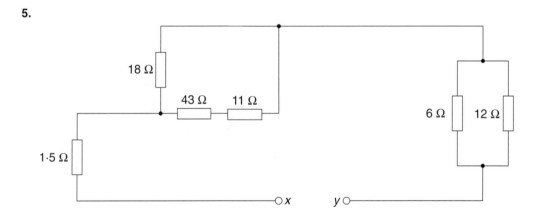

4.

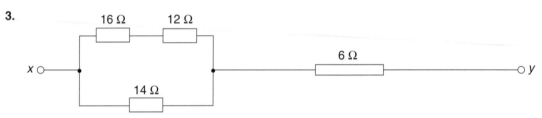

5.

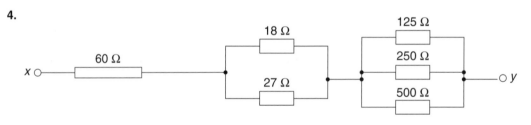

OHM'S LAW (Basic Problems)

Find the unknown (V, I or R) in each of the circuits below.

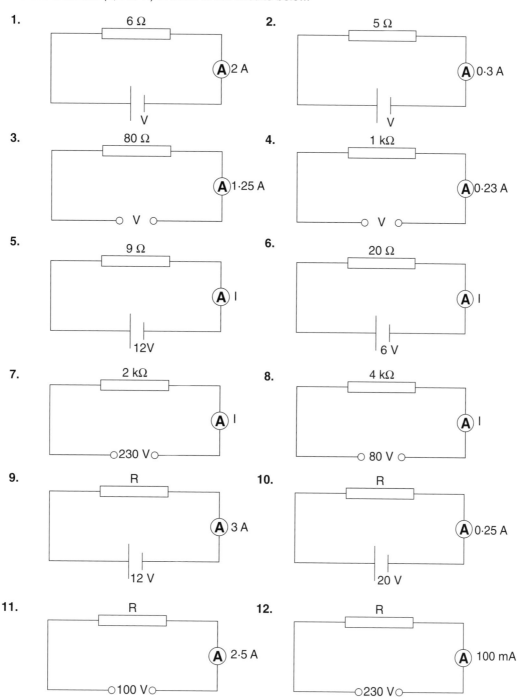

1. 6 Ω — (A) 2 A — V

2. 5 Ω — (A) 0·3 A — V

3. 80 Ω — (A) 1·25 A — V

4. 1 kΩ — (A) 0·23 A — V

5. 9 Ω — (A) I — 12V

6. 20 Ω — (A) I — 6 V

7. 2 kΩ — (A) I — 230 V

8. 4 kΩ — (A) I — 80 V

9. R — (A) 3 A — 12 V

10. R — (A) 0·25 A — 20 V

11. R — (A) 2·5 A — 100 V

12. R — (A) 100 mA — 230 V

OHM'S LAW (Intermediate Problems)

Find the readings on the meters in each of the circuits below.

1.

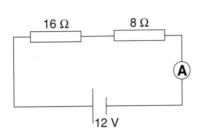

2.

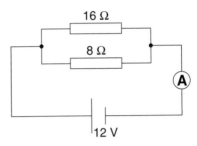

3.

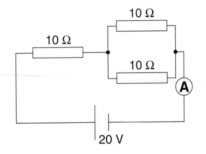

4.

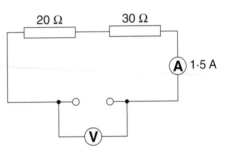

5.

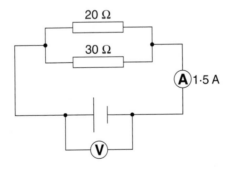

6.

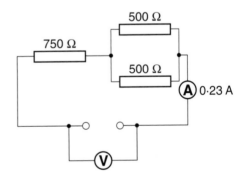

7.

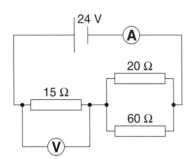

8.

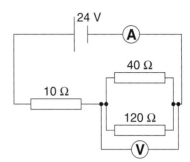

9.

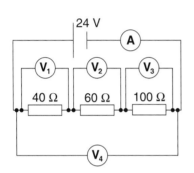

10.

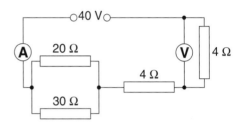

11.

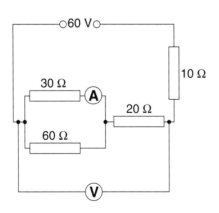

12.

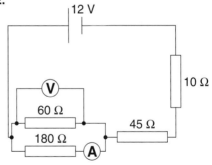

VOLTAGE DIVISION

Find the readings on each of the voltmeters in the circuits below.

1.

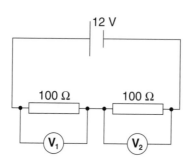

2.

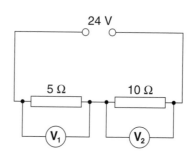

3.

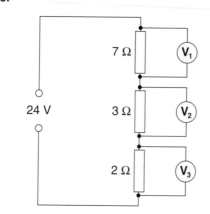

4.

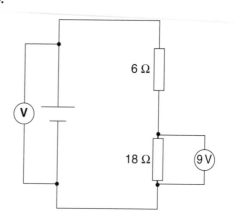

5.

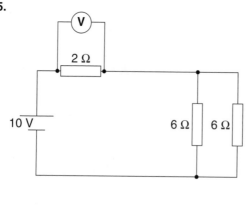

6.

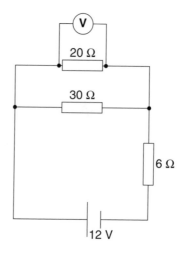

CURRENT DIVISION

Find the readings on each of the ammeters in the circuits below.

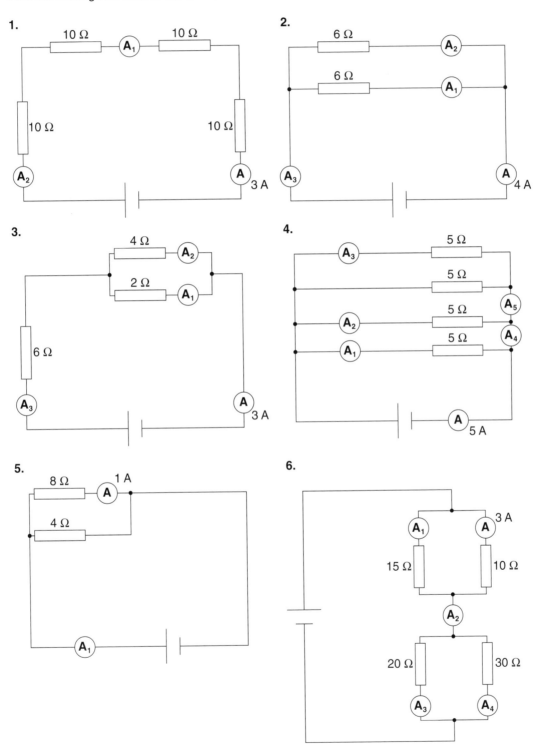

1.

10 Ω A_1 10 Ω

10 Ω   10 Ω

A_2 A   3 A

2.

6 Ω A_2

6 Ω A_1

A_3 A   4 A

3.

4 Ω A_2

2 Ω A_1

6 Ω

A_3 A   3 A

4.

A_3 5 Ω

5 Ω

A_2 5 Ω A_5

A_1 5 Ω A_4

A   5 A

5.

8 Ω   1 A   A

4 Ω

A_1

6.

A_1 A   3 A

15 Ω   10 Ω

A_2

20 Ω   30 Ω

A_3 A_4

POWER AND ELECTRICAL ENERGY

1. Calculate the power of

   (a) a 12 V car battery delivering a current of 3 A to a bulb,
   (b) a 230 V mains supply delivering 2·5 A to a fire,
   (c) a 230 V mains supply delivering 8 A to an electric kettle,
   (d) a 230 V mains supply delivering 0·40 A to an electric shaver.

2. Calculate the current drawn by

   (a) a 920 W hair dryer connected to a 230 V mains supply,
   (b) a 2·3 kW electric kettle connected to a 230 V mains supply,
   (c) a 100 W bulb connected to a 230 V mains supply,
   (d) a 48 W bulb connected to a 12 V car battery.

3. Calculate the voltage across a

   (a) 10 W resistor when the current is 0·5 A,
   (b) 24 W bulb when the current is 2 A,
   (c) 1150 W fire when the current is 5 A,
   (d) 0·1 W resistor when the current is 5 mA.

The following power problems require a knowledge of Ohm's Law.

4. An electric fire draws a 4 A current from the mains supply (230 V).

   (a) What is the power rating of the fire?
   (b) What is the resistance of the heater element?

5. A car headlamp bulb is rated at 48 W. If it is operated from the car battery (12 V) find

   (a) the current drawn from the battery,
   (b) the resistance of the bulb.

6. A special lighting tube has a power rating of 500 W. If it draws 4 A from its supply,

   (a) what is its supply voltage?
   (b) what is the resistance of the lighting tube?

7. A technician finds three bulbs in the store. Each bulb has a voltage and a current value written on it.

Bulb A	=	6 V	0·03 A
Bulb B	=	1·25 V	0·25 A
Bulb C	=	12 V	0·06 A

   (a) Calculate the power rating of each bulb.
   (b) Calculate the resistance of each bulb.

8. What is the resistance of a 60 W bulb operating from a 230 V supply?

9. What is the resistance of a 150 W bulb operating from a 230 V supply?

10. A 24 Ω resistor is connected across a 6 V battery.

    (a) What is the power rating of the resistor?

    (b) How many joules of electrical energy does it use in 10 s?

11. A 240 Ω resistor is connected across a 12 V battery.

    (a) What is the electrical power dissipated in the resistor?

    (b) How many joules of electrical energy does it use in 1 minute?

12. In the circuit shown find

    (a) the current in the circuit,

    (b) the power dissipated in the resistor.

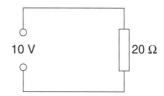

13. In the circuit find

    (a) the total resistance of the circuit,

    (b) the current flowing through each resistor,

    (c) the voltage across the 50 Ω resistor,

    (d) the power dissipated in the 50 Ω resistor,

    (e) the voltage across the 150 Ω resistor,

    (f) the power dissipated in the 150 Ω resistor.

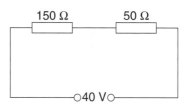

14. From the circuit shown find

    (a) the voltage across each resistor,

    (b) the power dissipated in each resistor.

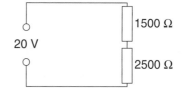

15. For each of the following three cases calculate

    (a) the power dissipated in the device,

    (b) the total energy consumed within 5 minutes.

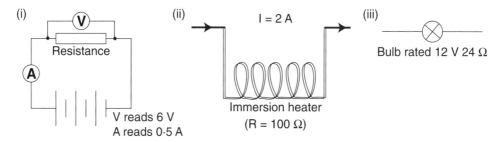

16. A cooker is rated at 4·6 kW when connected to a 230 V supply.

How much energy will it use in five minutes (assuming the cooker is drawing its maximum current)?

17. A 1 kW electric heater is left on for an hour.

    (a) How many joules of electric energy does it use?
    (b) How many joules are there in a kilowatt-hour?

18. The diagram shows a domestic lighting circuit operating from a 230 V mains supply.

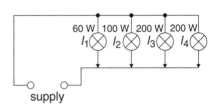

    (a) Find the current through each bulb (I_1, I_2, I_3, and I_4).
    (b) What is the current drawn from the mains supply?
    (c) What is the total power used in the circuit?

19. In the six circuits below, the fuses are very old. From boxes of fuses labelled 3A and 13A, choose the correct fuse for each circuit.

    (a)

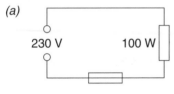

    (b)

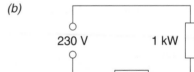

    (c)

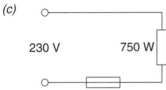

    (d)

    (e)

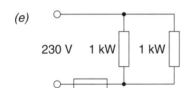

    (f)

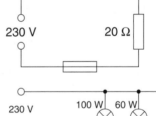

20. An electric fire has two 1 kW elements wired in parallel as shown in the circuit diagram.

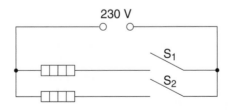

    (a) When only switch S_1 is closed, what is the current supplied?
    (b) When both switches are closed, what is the current from the mains supply?
    (c) The plug for the electric fire has a fuse in it. Should the value of the fuse be 3A or 13A?

21. Each bulb in the circuit below has "1·5 W, 0·25 A" stamped on it.

Assuming both bulbs are working normally, find the voltage of the battery.

22. The circuit below can be used to light a 4 V bulb using a 12 V supply.

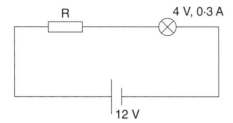

(a) For the bulb to operate normally, what is the potential difference across the resistor?
(b) Hence, calculate R.

23. In the circuit shown, R protects the bulb.

Calculate the value of R when the bulb is working normally.

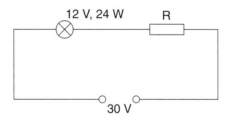

24. In the circuit shown below, bulb Y has a power rating of 12 W and draws a 2 A current. The current through bulb X is 1 A.

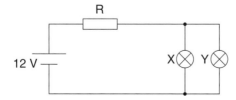

Calculate the resistance R in the circuit if bulbs X and Y are operating at their normal power rating.

SECTION 5

BEHIND THE WALL

The two circuits below are set up to make comparisons between a simple parallel circuit and a ring circuit. All the bulbs are identical.

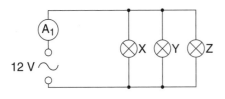 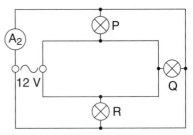

1. (a) If bulb X "blows", what happens to Y and Z?
    (b) If bulb P "blows", what happens to Q and R?

2. Consider the current from each supply.

    (a) Which ammeter has the greater current?
    (b) Why is the current in the other circuit less?

3. Write down two advantages of using the ring circuit in preference to the simple parallel circuit.

4. This circuit shows part of the wiring in a house.

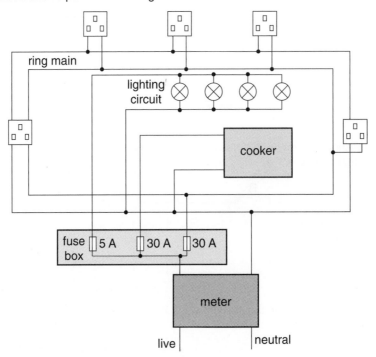

(a) How many circuits are shown?

(b) In a typical house there are ten 13 A points in the ring mains. Why is a 30 A fuse used to protect this circuit?

(c) The cooker is switched on using a large red switch on the kitchen wall. You do not plug in a cooker like an electric kettle. Why must the cooker be wired separately?

(d) What is the difference between wire used for the lighting circuit and the wire used for the ring mains?

5. John has a coil of wire wound round a nail. He connects both ends of the wire to a lab pack set at 12 V.

(i) When he switches on the lab pack a little black button pops out very quickly.

(ii) He switches the lab pack off.

(iii) He pushes the black button in.

(iv) He alters the voltage to 4 V.

(v) When he switches on the lab pack the black button stays in this time.

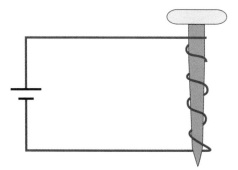

(a) Why did the black button pop out when the voltage was 12 V?

(b) Why did the black button not pop out when the voltage was 4 V?

(c) John's teacher tells him that the black button is a kind of fuse called a circuit breaker. A fuse is cheaper than a circuit breaker so what advantage does a circuit breaker have over a fuse?

THE KILOWATT HOUR

6. A 2 kW heater is switched on for five hours.

(a) How many kilowatt hours have been used?

(b) Calculate the cost at 8p per kW h.

7. A 5 kW immersion heater is switched on for four hours.

(a) How many kilowatt hours have been used?

(b) Calculate the cost at 8p per kW h.

8. A 200 W bulb has been left switched on all night (eight hours).

(a) How many kilowatt hours have been used?

(b) Calculate the cost at 8p per kW h.

9. A 2·4 kW electric kettle takes five minutes to boil.

    (a) How many kilowatt hours have been used?
    (b) Calculate the cost at 8p per kW h.

10. Which costs more to run:

    a 100 W bulb switched on for 4·5 hours or a 1200 W heater switched on for 30 minutes?

    All working must be shown. Take the cost of 1 kW h to be 8p.

SECTION 6

MOVEMENT FROM ELECTRICITY

1. The diagram shows the magnetic field around a bar magnet.

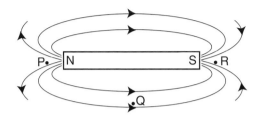

Copy and complete the following statements.

(a) Lines of force travel from .... to ....
(b) The magnetic field at point .... is stronger than at point ....
(c) Points .... and .... have the same magnetic field strength.

2. Oersted discovered that passing a current through a wire produces a magnetic field round the wire.

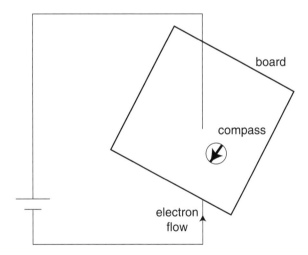

(a) Copy the board and draw the magnetic field round the wire.

(b) What would happen to the compass if the battery was disconnected?

3. Louise wants to make an electromagnet which is strong enough to lift a toy car. She uses the following circuit.

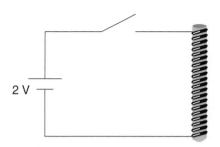

2 V

Coil is 20 turns wound round a hollow cardboard tube.

The coil will pick up some paper clips but it is too weak to pick up the car. Given any additional apparatus you may require, show Louise three methods of increasing the field strength of the electromagnet.

4. A reed relay uses two metal contacts with a very small gap between them.

(a) What happens to this gap when S is closed?

(b) When S is closed, what does the solenoid produce?

(c) Give an example of a circuit which uses a reed relay.

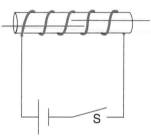

S

5. A piece of copper wire is rested upon two metal "runners" like a railway track and placed between the poles of a large horseshoe magnet as shown in the diagram. When the switch is closed, the piece of copper wire shoots along the two runners until it gets out of the magnetic field.

(a) Explain what is happening to the piece of copper.

(b) If the battery terminals were reversed, which way would the copper wire move?

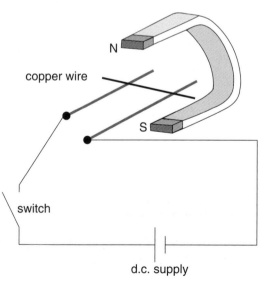

copper wire

N

S

switch

d.c. supply

6.   A thin piece of aluminium foil is placed between the poles of a magnet and a d.c. current is passed through it.

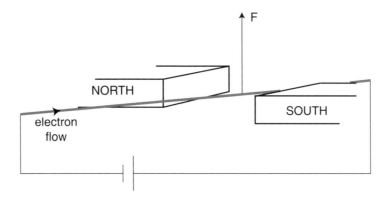

The foil experiences a force and jumps upwards (see diagram).

(a)   If the current in the aluminium foil was reversed, what would happen to the force acting on the foil?

(b)   With the electron flow as shown in the diagram, the north and south poles are reversed. Which way would the foil jump?

7.   The diagram illustrates the basic principle of the d.c. electric motor.

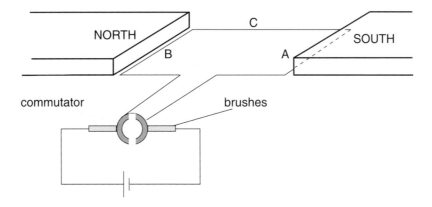

Consider the direction of flow of current in the sides A, B and C of the loop of wire. The force on side A is upwards.

(a)   In which direction is the force on side B?
(b)   What is the force acting on side C?

8. The diagram below shows a single coil in an electric motor.

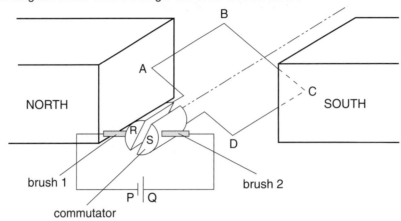

R is in contact with brush 1.

(a) Use all the letters in the diagram to trace the path of electron flow around the circuit.

The coil rotates until R is in contact with brush 2.

(b) Use all the letters in the diagram to trace the path of electron flow round the circuit this time.

9. By making reference to the diagram in question 8:

(a) Explain the function of the commutator.

(b) The brushes are fixed in position but must make good contact with both halves of the commutator. What properties does **carbon** have that makes it ideal for the brushes?

10. In commercial motors:

(a) Why are field coils used in place of permanent magnets?

(b) Why is there a number of rotating coils instead of only one?

UNIT 3

HEALTH PHYSICS

SECTION 1

THE USE OF THERMOMETERS

1. A student examines two mercury thermometers. All numbers refer to temperature in degrees Centigrade.

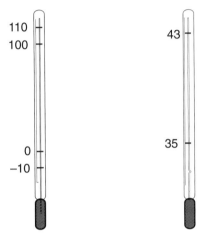

Laboratory Thermometer   Clinical Thermometer

(a) What is the range of the laboratory thermometer?

(b) What is the range of the clinical thermometer?

(c) Which one is used to measure the temperature of boiling water?

(d) Suggest a use for the other thermometer.

2. Both clinical and laboratory thermometers are sitting in a beaker of water at 40 °C.

They are removed at exactly the same time.

(a) What happens to the laboratory thermometer?

(b) What happens to the clinical thermometer?

(c) What is the purpose of the "kink" in the tube of the clinical thermometer?

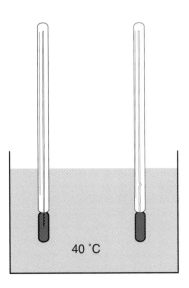

40 °C

3. A liquid crystal strip thermometer is often used to take a baby's temperature.

   (a) How is it used?

   (b) Why is it preferred to a clinical thermometer?

4. A simple fire alarm uses a bimetallic strip.

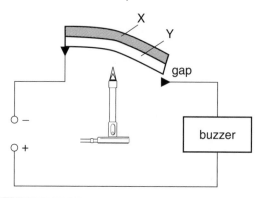

   (a) Copy and complete the following sentences.
           When the bimetallic strip is heated, both metals ....
           Copper expands .... than iron so the strip bends and closes the ....
           The circuit is now .... and the buzzer sounds.

   (b) Which one is the copper, X or Y?

5. Mercury thermometer, alcohol thermometer, digital thermometer or rototherm — which one uses the principal of the bimetallic strip?

6. Every thermometer requires some physical property that changes with temperature. Study the table below and match up the type of thermometer to the correct variable.

Type of thermometer	Variable
Rototherm	length of liquid column
Mercury	voltage
Thermocouple	angle of deflection

SECTION 2

USING SOUND

1. You are swimming underwater at a swimming pool. The attendant blows a whistle.

    (a) Can you hear the sound?

    (b) Can sound travel through water?

    (c) Can sound travel through a gas?

    (d) Can sound travel through a solid?

2. In a Western movie, a cowboy suspects he is being followed by Indians. He stops and listens carefully but hears nothing. He dismounts and listens to the ground and hears the steady drumming of horses' hooves behind him.

    Why does sound travel better through a solid than it does through a gas?

3. Copy the diagram of the stethoscope and label the parts A, B, C and D.

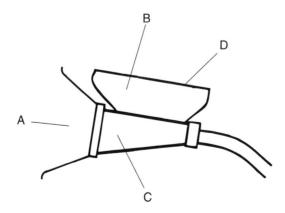

4. John found that his little sister had cut up his notes on the stethoscope.

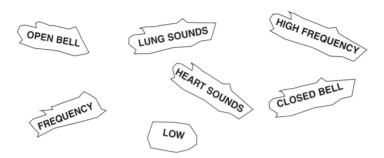

Starting with OPEN BELL, rewrite John's notes to describe how the stethoscope works.

5. A doctor uses a stethoscope to listen to a patient. The wavelength of the sound he hears is 4·25 m.

   (a) Calculate the frequency of this sound ($v = 340$ m/s).

   (b) Is the doctor listening to the heart or lungs?

   (c) Is the doctor using the closed bell or the open bell?

6. A ship can be used to find the depth of the sea by reflecting ultrasound off the sea bed.

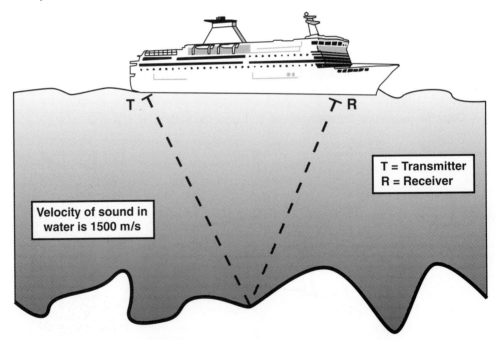

The time between the transmitted and reflected signals is 0·4 s.

   (a) How far did the sound travel?

   (b) What was the depth of the sea?

7. A technician on board the ship in question 6 is looking at an oscilloscope screen. He sees a transmitted signal and a reflected signal.

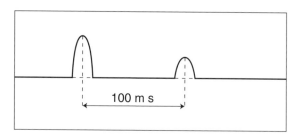

100 m s

(a) Why is the reflected signal smaller?

(b) Use the information on the screen to calculate how far the sound travelled ($v = 1500$ m/s).

(c) How deep is the sea at this point?

8. Equipment such as this in questions 6 and 7 was used to hunt for the Loch Ness Monster.

If "Nessie" swam under the ship, draw the new picture the technician would see.

9. Ultrasound is used to measure the depth of a baby in its mother's womb. The speed of ultrasound in human tissue is 1500 m/s. The time between transmission and the reflected signal is 1×10^{-4} seconds.

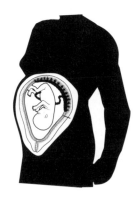

(a) How far did the sound travel?

(b) How deep is the part of the baby which caused this reflection?

10. Another part of the baby in question 9 produces a reflected signal $1 \cdot 6 \times 10^{-5}$ seconds after transmission.

(a) How deep is this part of the baby?

(b) Why is ultrasound used to scan for the baby in preference to X-rays?

11. The numbers 130, 110, 90 and 60 are missing from the table below. Copy the table and fill in the missing numbers.

Sound	Noise level dB
Pop group at 1 m	
Heavy truck	
Jet engine	
Normal conversation at 1 m	

12. What is the pain threshold in decibels?

13. What is the frequency range of human hearing?

14. An ultrasonic whistle is used to call a dog.

(a) Is the frequency of the sound 10 kHz, 18 kHz or 22 kHz?

(b) Calculate the wavelength of the ultrasound (velocity of sound in air is 340 m/s).

15. The dog in question 14 hears the ultrasound 0·75 s after the whistle sounds.

(a) How far away is the dog?

(b) If the dog runs back at 10 m/s, how long will it take to return?

SECTION 3

LIGHT AND SIGHT

1. Light slows down when it enters glass.

   Copy and complete the diagram by marking in:

   (a) the angle of incidence;

   (b) the angle of refraction;

   (c) the normal.

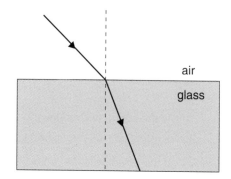

2. Copy and complete the following diagrams showing what happens to the light in the glass and after it has passed through.

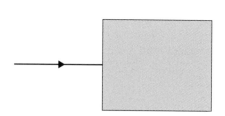

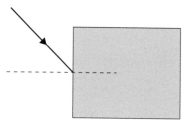

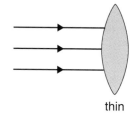

thin

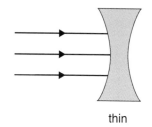

thin

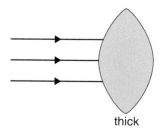

thick

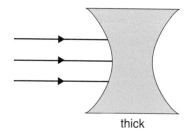

thick

3.   Copy the diagram and complete it to show how the image is formed inside the eye.

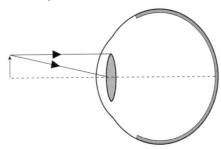

(a)   Is the image upside down?

(b)   If the object was the letter A draw the equivalent image.

(c)   If the object was the letter F draw the equivalent image.

4.   A man goes into the optician complaining he can no longer read the newspaper.

(a)   Is he long or short sighted?

(b)   Can he identify players at a football match?

5.   In a driving test, a woman is failed because she cannot read a distant number plate.

(a)   Is she long or short sighted?

(b)   Can she read the *Highway Code*?

6.   A person with **perfect vision** is able to focus light from a distant object (or a near object) on to the retina by changing the shape of the lens.

distant object   near object

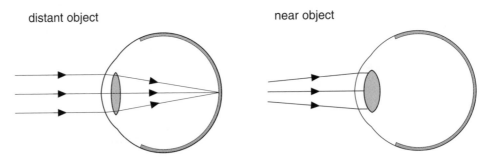

(a)   Copy and complete the diagram for the near object showing where the light focuses.

(b)   Which lens is stronger?

7. Copy and complete the two diagrams below for a person who is **long sighted**.

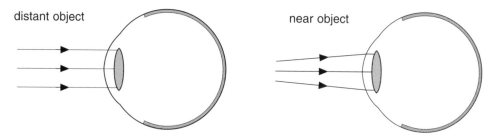

8. Copy and complete the two diagrams below for a person who is **short sighted**.

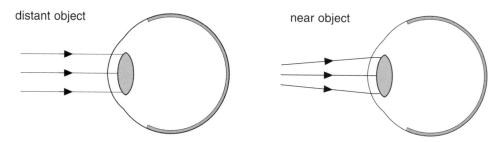

9. The correction for **long sight** involves adding a lens to work in conjunction with the lens inside the eye.

Copy and complete the diagram by drawing in the missing lens and the paths of the three rays.

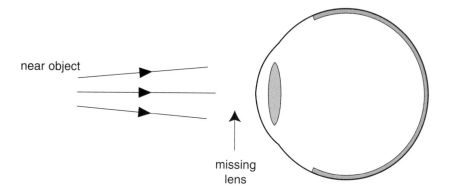

10. The correction for **short sight** involves adding a lens to work in conjunction with the lens inside the eye.

Copy and complete the diagram by drawing in the missing lens and the paths of the three rays.

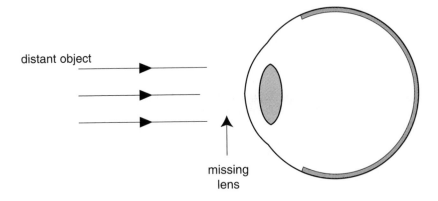

POWER OF A LENS

1. The focal length of a convex lens is 20 cm.

Calculate the power of the lens.

2. The focal length of a convex lens is 30 cm.
Calculate the power of the lens.

3. *(a)* A convex lens focuses parallel light in 5 cm. Calculate the power of the lens.

    (b) A convex lens focuses parallel light in 10 cm. Calculate the power of the lens.

    (c) Which lens is thicker?

4. The focal length of a concave lens is –20 cm.

Calculate the power of the lens.

5. The focal length of a concave lens is –25 cm.

Calculate the power of the lens.

6. *(a)* A concave lens has a power of –10 D. Calculate the focal length of the lens.

    (b) A concave lens has a power of –4 D. Calculate the focal length of the lens.

    (c) Which lens is thicker?

7. A lens has a power of +4 D.

    (a) Calculate the focal length of the lens.

    (b) Is the lens convex or concave?

8. A lens has a power of –8 D.

    (a) Calculate the focal length of the lens.

    (b) Is the lens convex or concave?

USE OF FIBRE OPTICS IN MEDICINE

1. Copy the diagram and draw the path of the light ray until it emerges from the optical fibre.

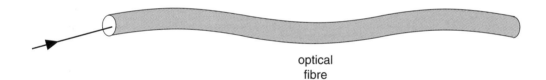

optical
fibre

2. If light travels at 2×10^8 m/s inside an optical fibre, how long will it take to travel 3 m?

3. An endoscope has two bundles of optical fibres.
    What is each one for?

4. A doctor uses an endoscope as an exploratory tool.
    Why is this preferable to a surgical exploratory operation?

5. One advantage of the endoscope is that it transmits "cold light". However, it still depends on a filament lamp.

    (a) Explain how the light is cold.
    (b) Why is cold light important inside the patient?

SECTION 4

USING THE SPECTRUM

1.   What type of laser would a doctor use to vaporise a tumour that is blocking air to the lungs?

2.   If the tumour in question 1 was in the oesophagus,

   (a)   could the doctor reach it with the laser without cutting the patient?

   (b)   what additional equipment would the doctor require?

3.   The carbon dioxide laser is sometimes referred to as a laser scalpel.

   (a)   What is a laser scalpel?

   (b)   Why use a carbon dioxide laser?

4.   An eye surgeon uses a laser beam to photocoagulate blood vessels in the retina.

   (a)   What type of laser should he use?

   (b)   What is photocoagulation?

   (c)   The patient is now much less likely to go blind. Precisely why?

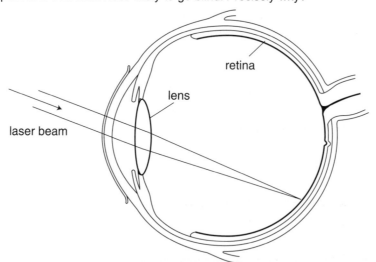

5.   If a laser produces 1200 J of energy in 1 minute, calculate the power of the laser.

6.   During a visit to a university, Cynthia was shown round the laser laboratories. The walls were painted matt black. Even the ceiling was matt black. Cynthia liked the colour scheme! This painting is a safety feature.

   Explain to Cynthia why everything is in black.

7. What is used to detect X-rays?

8. Would a crack in a bone appear black or white on an X-ray?

9. What advantage does a C.A.T. scanner have over a simple X-ray?

10. *(a)* One X-ray has a frequency of 5×10^{15} Hz. Calculate the wavelength of the X-ray.

    (b) Another X-ray has a frequency of 9×10^{15} Hz. Calculate the wavelength of this X-ray.

    (c) Which of the two X-rays has the greater energy?

11. People in hospital for long periods of time benefit from regular doses of U.V. radiation. What does the U.V. radiation do?

12. Sunbathers on the beach put on lotion to protect them from sunburn.
    What other skin disease could be caused by excessive amounts of U.V. radiation?

13. *(a)* One U.V. wave has a wavelength of 300 nm. Calculate the frequency of this wave.

    (b) Another U.V. wave has a wavelength of 350 nm. Calculate the frequency of this wave.

    (c) Which of the two waves has the greater energy?

14. Following an earthquake, a fireman uses an infrared camera to search for survivors trapped under the rubble.

    (a) What waves will the camera detect?

    (b) The fireman detects a "hot spot".
    (i)   Could it be a dog?   (ii)   Could it be a child?

15. In a film, an alien is hunting Arnold Swarzenegger by using infrared radiation.

    (a) Where are the infrared rays coming from?

    At one point in the film, "Arnie" is covered in mud.

    (b) Can the alien detect him?

    (c) Give a reason for your answer.

16. An infrared camera is used to film foxes coming into a town at night.
    Will the camera detect the street lights?

17. *(a)* What is a thermogram?

    (b) What would a tumour look like on a thermogram?

18. *(a)* One infrared wave has a wavelength of 4×10^{-6} m. Calculate the frequency of this wave.

    (b) Another infrared wave has a wavelength of $4 \cdot 5 \times 10^{-6}$ m. Calculate the frequency of this wave.

    (c) Which of the two waves has the greater energy?

SECTION 5

NUCLEAR RADIATION — HUMANS AND MEDICINE

1. The symbol for sodium is $^{23}_{11}$Na. An atom of sodium looks like this.

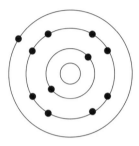

    (a) How many protons does it have?

    (b) How many electrons does it have?

    (c) How many neutrons does it have?

    (d) What is the name given to the central core which contains the protons and neutrons?

2. *(a)* Considering the sodium atom above has both positive and negative particles, explain why it is uncharged.

    (b) If an electron is removed from the sodium atom, what charge does it have?

3. *(a)* What is meant by ionisation?

    (b) "The ionising power of an alpha particle is much greater than that of a beta particle." Explain the above statement with particular reference to speed and charge.

4. Copy and complete the following table for the three types of radiation.

Type	Description	Mass	Charge
α	Helium nucleus 2p + 2n		
β			
γ			

5.   The top view of a cloud chamber is shown below. The source of radiation is placed at point S in the middle of the chamber.

The source is known to emit alpha particles and beta particles and from the diagram it is obvious that two different types of particle are being emitted. The thickness of the track is a measure of the ionisation it produces.

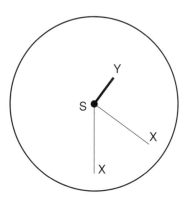

Copy and complete the sentences below.

Track X represents a .... particle.

Track Y represents a .... particle.

Track X is long and thin because ....

Track Y is short and thick because ....

6.   In a cloud chamber experiment using an old cloud chamber, a radioactive substance shows two different tracks (similar to those in question 3) but the substance is known to emit three different kinds of radiation.

   (a)   What kind of radiation is not detected by the cloud chamber?

   (b)   Suggest an explanation of this result.

7.   The diagram below is the cut away view of a Geiger-Muller tube. For every discharge inside the tube there is a pulse of current which registers 1 count on the scalar counter.

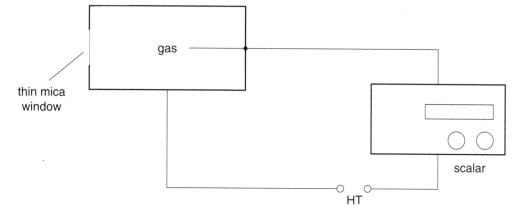

   (a)   Why is the window very thin?

   (b)   Is the gas at low or high pressure?

   (c)   What kind of gas is normally used?

   (d)   Explain in detail how the discharge occurs (making reference to the avalanche process).

8. George Curie, a teacher at Radium High School, had just finished an experiment using a Geiger counter and put all the radioactive sources in a safe place. When he came back to the Geiger counter, which was still switched on, he noticed that it still counted from time to time even though no radioactive source was present. Suggest an explanation for his observation.

9. Alpha, beta and gamma radiations can be separated by an electric field.

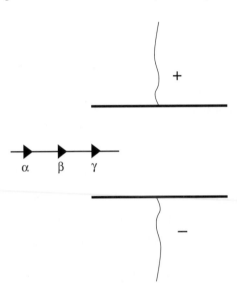

Copy and complete the diagram showing what happens to each radiation.

10. Rewrite the sentence below filling in the blank spaces.

.... can be stopped by a sheet of paper while .... will be stopped by 2 cm of aluminium but .... can penetrate several centimetres of lead.

HALF-LIFE

1. What is meant by the half-life of a radioactive source?

2. A radioactive source has a count rate of 160 counts per minute (excluding background count rate). If the half-life of the source is four days, what will the count rate be after
    (a) 4 days?
    (b) 8 days?
    (c) 12 days?
    (d) How long will it take for the count rate to fall to 5 counts per minute?

3. A radioactive source has a count rate of 128 counts per minute (excluding background count rate). If the half-life of the source is six days, what will the count rate be after
    (a) 6 days?
    (b) 12 days?
    (c) 18 days?
    (d) How long will it take for the count rate to fall to 4 counts per minute?

4. A radioactive source has a count rate of 80 counts per minute (excluding background count rate).
    (a) If the half-life of the source is 5 days, what will the count rate be after
        (i)   5 days,   (ii)   10 days,   (iii)   15 days,   (iv)   20 days?
    (b) Plot a graph of count rate against time for these results.
    (c) Use the graph to find the count rate after
        (i)   12 days,   (ii)   18 days.

5. A radioactive source has a count rate of 200 counts per minute (excluding background count rate).
    (a) If the half-life of the source is 12 days, what will the count rate be after
        (i)   12 days,   (ii)   24 days,   (iii)   36 days,   (iv)   48 days?
    (b) Plot a graph of count rate against time for these results.
    (c) Use the graph to find the count rate after
        (i)   16 days,   (ii)   40 days.

6. A radioactive source has a count rate of 240 counts per minute (excluding background count rate).
    (a) If the half-life of the source is 18 days, what will the count rate be after
        (i)   18 days,   (ii)   36 days,   (iii)   54 days,   (iv)   72 days?
    (b) Plot a graph of count rate against time for these results.
    (c) Use the graph to find the count rate after
        (i)   40 days,   (ii)   9 days.

7. In an experiment to measure half-life, the table of results below was obtained. Readings were taken every two days.

Time / days	Corrected count rate / min
start	130
2	85
4	55
6	38
8	24

Plot a graph of corrected count rate against time and hence find the half-life of the source.

8. After 24 days, a radioactive source shows a count rate of 9 counts per minute (excluding background count rate).

If the half-life of the source is 6 days, what was the original count rate at the start of timing?

9. A source initially has an activity of 160 kBq (corrected) and this drops to 20 kBq (corrected) in 1 hour.

What is the half-life of the source?

10. A frozen body was discovered in the Alps. A scientist used carbon dating to find the age of the remains. The half-life of carbon 14 is approximately 5600 years.

A sample from the frozen body was measured at 15 counts per minute (corrected).

An identical modern sample was measured at 30 counts per minute (corrected).

(a) How old was the frozen body?

(b) The count from another archaelogical find was 7·5 counts per minute (corrected). How old was this find?

OVERVIEW

1. An electronic system consists of three parts.

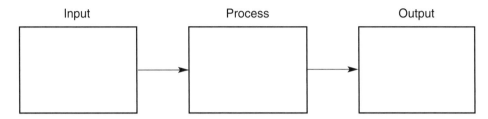

Input   Process   Output

   (a) Copy the three boxes and fill in the three parts of the system for a school public address system.
   (b) Repeat *(a)* for a personal stereo system.

2. A mercury in glass thermometer has an analogue output.
   What is meant by the word analogue?

3. A digital thermometer with a whole number display has a digital output.
   What is meant by the word digital?

4. Study the oscilloscope picture.
   Is it analogue or digital?

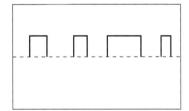

5. Copy and complete the oscilloscope picture to show what an analogue signal would look like.

SECTION 2

OUTPUT DEVICES

1. State the energy change in each of the following output devices.
    (a) Loudspeaker.
    (b) Electric motor.
    (c) Solenoid.
    (d) Relay.
    (e) L.E.D.

2. Draw a table with two columns labelled "Analogue" and "Digital". Classify the five output devices in question 1 into analogue or digital.

3. What output device would you use for:
    (a) a baby alarm system;
    (b) a power-on indicator for a laboratory pack;
    (c) a time-lock bolt;
    (d) a calculator display.

4. *(a)* Draw the symbol for an L.E.D.
    (b) The circuit below shows a gap where an L.E.D. should be.

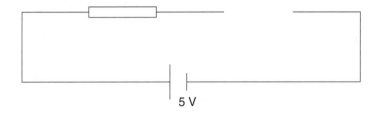

5 V

    Copy and complete the circuit by adding in the L.E.D. (careful).

5. Why does the L.E.D. in question 4*(b)* need a resistor connected in series with it?

6. A diode is rated at 2 V, 100 mA (maximum), so it needs to be protected from a 5 V supply by using a series resistor.

   (a) What is the voltage across R?

   (b) Calculate the size of the protective resistor (R) required.

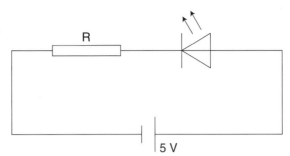

7. A diode is rated at 1·0 V, 50 mA (maximum), so it needs a protective resistor in the circuit shown.

   (a) What is the voltage across R?

   (b) Calculate the size of the protective resistor (R) required.

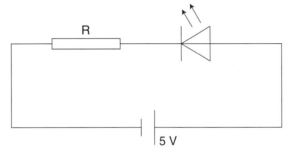

8. A diode is rated at 1·2 V, 20 mA (maximum), so it needs a protective resistor in the circuit shown.

   Calculate the size of R required to protect the diode.

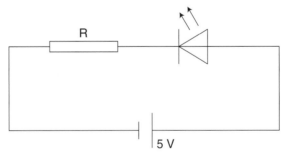

9. The diagram shows a 7-segment display. Each segment is labelled with a letter.

Which segments would be lit to make the number

(a) 6,

(b) 5,

(c) 0?

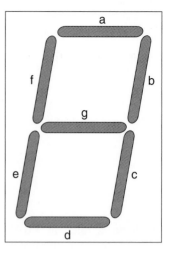

10. Copy and complete the table below by filling in the decimal equivalent of the binary numbers given.

Binary	Decimal
0 0 0 0	0
0 0 0 1	
0 0 1 0	
0 0 1 1	
0 1 0 0	
0 1 0 1	
1 0 0 0	
1 0 0 1	

SECTION 3

INPUT DEVICES

Thermistors and L.D.Rs.

1. What are the energy changes in
    (a) a microphone,
    (b) a thermocouple,
    (c) a solar cell?

2. A thermistor at a certain temperature has a current of 20 mA passing through it. If the voltage across it is 3 V, calculate the resistance of the thermistor.

3. An L.D.R. at a certain light level has a current of 10 mA passing through it. If the voltage across it is 2 V, calculate the resistance of the L.D.R.

4. The thermistor in the circuit shown has a resistance of 240 Ω when the temperature is 20 °C.

    (a) Calculate the current in the thermistor.

    (b) When heated to 100 °C, the resistance drops to 60 Ω. Calculate the current now.

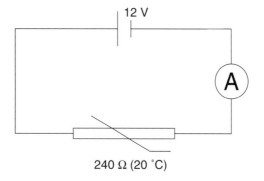

240 Ω (20 °C)

5. The L.D.R. in the circuit shown has a resistance of 1200 Ω when the light level is 200 units.

    (a) Calculate the current in the L.D.R.

    (b) When the light level is increased to 800 units, the resistance drops to 75 Ω. Calculate the current now.

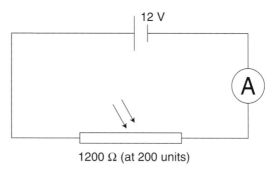

1200 Ω (at 200 units)

6. The thermistor in the circuit shown has a resistance of 5000 Ω (at 20 ˚C).

Calculate the current in the circuit (at 20 ˚C).

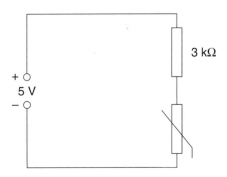

7. The L.D.R. in the circuit shown has a resistance of 10 kΩ (in daylight).

Calculate the current in the circuit (in daylight).

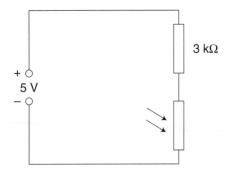

8. If the thermistor in the circuit shown below has a resistance of 3000 Ω at 60 ˚C, calculate the output voltage (at 60 ˚C).

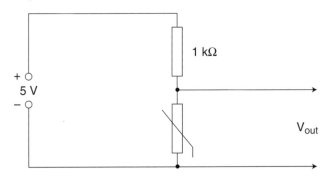

9. If the thermistor in the circuit shown below has a resistance of 3000 Ω at 60 ˚C, calculate the output voltage (at 60 ˚C).

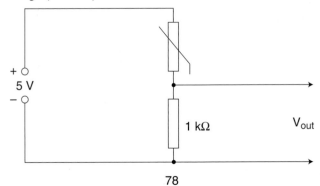

10. Study the data table for the L.D.R. in the circuit shown below.

Conditions	Resistance / kΩ
Daylight	10
Darkness	500

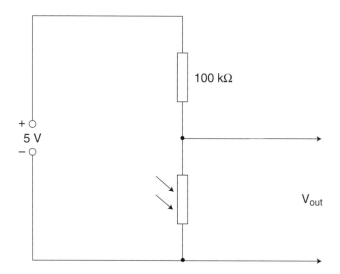

Calculate the output voltage

(a) in daylight,

(b) in darkness.

Capacitor circuits

1. A capacitor stores charge. What else does it store?

2. When the switch is closed, the capacitor charges up. When the capacitor is fully charged,

(a) what is the reading on the voltmeter?

(b) what is the reading on the ammeter?

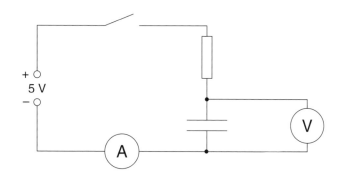

3.　When the switch is closed, the capacitor charges up.

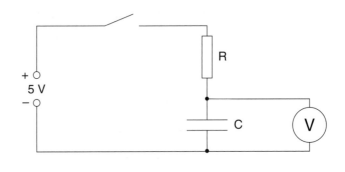

(a)　When the capacitor is fully charged, what is the voltage across it?

(b)　When the capacitor is fully charged, what is the voltage across R?

4.　When the switch is closed, the reading on the voltmeter builds up to 5 V in 10 seconds.

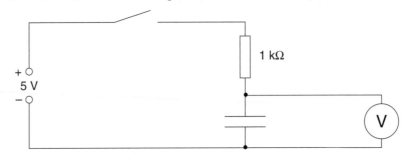

(a)　When the resistor is replaced with a 10 kΩ resistor, the time taken for the voltmeter to reach 5 V is

　　　10 s,　　　less than 10 s,　　　greater than 10 s.

(b)　When the resistor is replaced with a 100 Ω resistor, the time taken for the voltmeter to reach 5 V is

　　　10 s,　　　less than 10 s,　　　greater than 10 s.

5.　When the switch is closed, the reading on the voltmeter builds up to 5 V in 9 seconds.

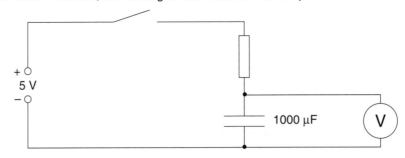

(a)　When the capacitor is replaced with a 220 μF capacitor, the time taken for the voltmeter to reach 5 V is

　　　9 s,　　　less than 9 s,　　　greater than 9 s.

(b)　When the capacitor is replaced with a 1500 μF capacitor, the time taken for the voltmeter to reach 5 V is

　　　9 s,　　　less than 9 s,　　　greater than 9 s.

6. How could you design a delay circuit to take a picture and still have time to get into the picture?

7. When the switch is closed, the capacitor charges up. The graph shows how long the capacitor takes to charge.

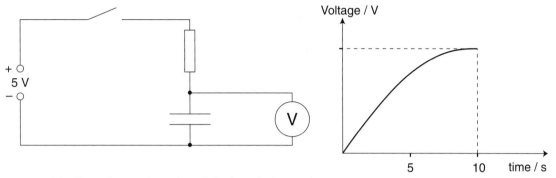

(a) Copy the graph and mark in the missing scale.

(b) Extend the graph to 15 s.

(c) Why is the graph shown not a straight line from the origin?

Voltage Dividers — A

Find the reading on the voltmeter in each of the following circuits.

1.

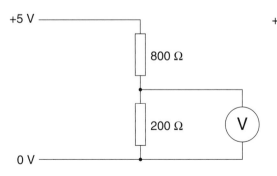

2.

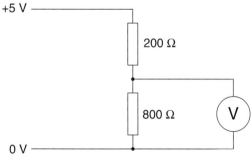

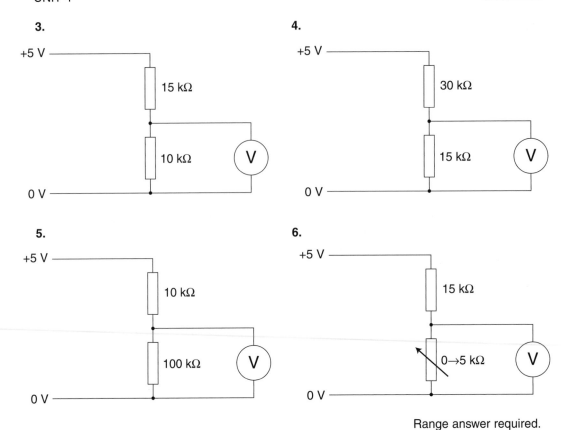

3.

+5 V ——

15 kΩ

10 kΩ   (V)

0 V ——

4.

+5 V ——

30 kΩ

15 kΩ   (V)

0 V ——

5.

+5 V ——

10 kΩ

100 kΩ   (V)

0 V ——

6.

+5 V ——

15 kΩ

0→5 kΩ   (V)

0 V ——

Range answer required.

Voltage Dividers — B

Copy and complete the passage under each circuit by filling in the missing words with **increases** or **decreases**.

1.

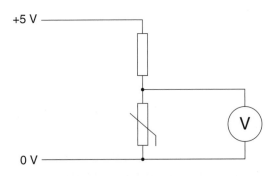

+5 V ——

(V)

0 V ——

When the temperature increases, the resistance of the thermistor decreases.
Therefore fraction of R_T (across thermistor) ....
Therefore voltmeter reading ....

2.

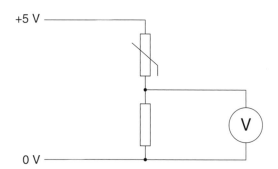

When the temperature increases, the resistance of the thermistor ....
Therefore fraction of R_T (across thermistor) ....
Therefore fraction of R_T (across resistor) ....
Therefore voltmeter reading ....

3.

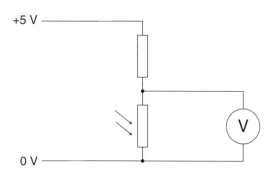

When the light intensity increases, the resistance of L.D.R. ....
Therefore fraction of R_T (across L.D.R) ....
Therefore voltmeter reading ....

4.

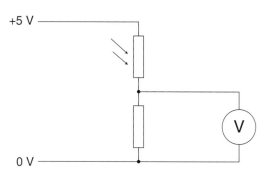

When the light intensity increases, the resistance of L.D.R. ....
Therefore fraction of R_T (across L.D.R) ....
Therefore fraction of R_T (across resistor) ....
Therefore voltmeter reading ....

SECTION 4

DIGITAL PROCESSES

The Transistor as a Switch

Copy and complete the passage next to each circuit by filling in the missing words with **increases** or **decreases**.

1.

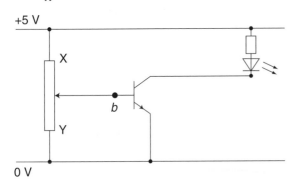

When the slider is moved to Y, the voltage level of point *b* ....
The transistor is switched ON / OFF.

2.

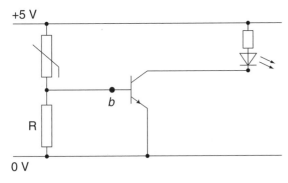

When the temperature increases, the resistance of the thermistor decreases.
Therefore voltage across thermistor ....
Therefore voltage across R ....
Therefore voltage level of point *b* ....
The transistor is switched ON / OFF.

3.

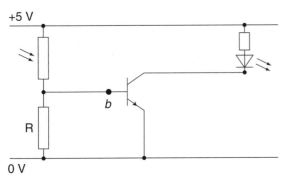

When the light intensity increases, the resistance of the L.D.R. ....
Therefore voltage across L.D.R ....
Therefore voltage across R ....
Therefore voltage level of point *b* ....
The transistor is switched ON / OFF.

4. Closing S discharges the capacitor. When S is opened, the capacitor charges up.

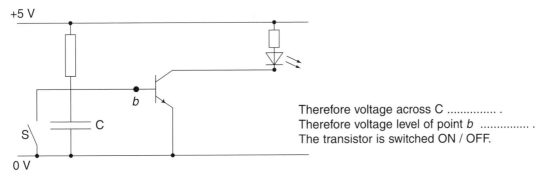

Therefore voltage across C ....
Therefore voltage level of point *b* ....
The transistor is switched ON / OFF.

Logic Gates

1. Copy and complete the truth table for the AND gate.

A	B	OUTPUT
0	0	
0	1	
1	0	
1	1	

2. Copy and complete the truth table for the OR gate.

A	B	OUTPUT
0	0	
0	1	
1	0	
1	1	

3. Copy and complete the truth table for the NOT gate.

INPUT	OUTPUT
0	
1	

For each of questions 4, 5, 6, 7 and 8, copy and complete the truth tables showing the combinational logic.

4.

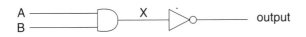

A	B	X	OUTPUT
0	0		
0	1		
1	0		
1	1		

5.

 output

A	B	OUTPUT
0	0	
0	1	
1	0	
1	1	

6.

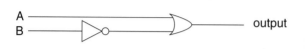 output

A	B	OUTPUT
0	0	
0	1	
1	0	
1	1	

7.

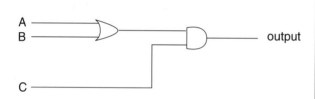 output

A	B	C	OUTPUT
0	0	0	
0	0	1	
0	1	0	
1	0	0	
0	1	1	
1	0	1	
1	1	0	
1	1	1	

8.

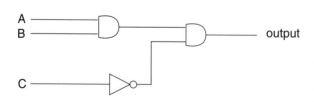 output

A	B	C	OUTPUT
0	0	0	
0	0	1	
0	1	0	
1	0	0	
0	1	1	
1	0	1	
1	1	0	
1	1	1	

9. Study the combinational logic circuit below.

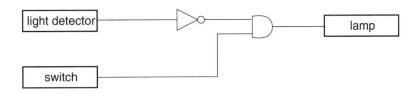

   (a) Under what conditions will the lamp come on?
   (b) Suggest a use for this circuit.

10. Thomas wants to design a circuit so that an alarm comes on either if it becomes dark or the temperature becomes too hot.

Thomas builds this circuit and then gives up!

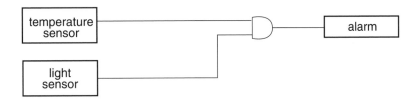

Using any additional equipment normally found in an electronics kit, copy and correct Thomas's circuit.

The Clock Pulse Generator

1. Examine the circuit for a clock pulse generator.

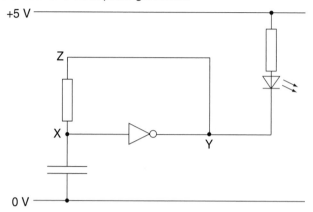

(a) Initally the capacitor is uncharged (copy and complete):
∴   voltage at X = 0;
∴   voltage level at Y =

(b) The capacitor now charges up (copy and complete):
∴   voltage at X =
∴   logic level at Y =
∴   voltage at Z =

(c) Will the capacitor now discharge?

2. Referring to the circuit in question 1, explain how the circuit produces pulses.

3. Referring to the circuit in question 1, the capacitor is replaced with one of larger capacitance.
(a) Does it take a longer or shorter time to charge?
(b) What does this do to the frequency of the pulses?

4. Referring to the circuit in question 1, the resistor (between X and Z) is replaced with one of larger resistance.
(a) Does the capacitor take a longer or shorter time to charge?
(b) What does this do to the frequency of the pulses?

5. The output of a counter circuit is
      analogue,   digital,   decimal?

SECTION 5

ANALOGUE PROCESSES

1. In a radio circuit,
    (a) what is the purpose of the amplifier?
    (b) where does the amplifier get its power?

2. A public address system has a C.R.O. connected across the input and another connected across the output.

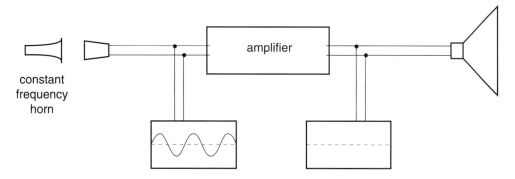

    Copy and complete the missing C.R.O. trace showing the signal after amplification.

3. Comparing the input and output signals in question 2,
    (a) is the frequency the same before and after amplification?
    (b) is the amplitude the same before and after amplification?

Voltage gain

4. What is the voltage gain in an amplifier if the voltage in is 2 V and the voltage out is 30 V?

5. What is the voltage gain in an amplifier if the voltage in is 0·5 V and the voltage out is 10 V?

6. What is the voltage gain in an amplifier if the voltage in is 100 mV and the voltage out is 5 V?

7. The voltage gain of an operational amplifier is 10. Calculate the output voltage if the input voltage is 0·8 V.

8. The voltage gain of an operational amplifier is 20. Calculate the input voltage if the output voltage is 8 V.

Use $P = \dfrac{V^2}{R}$ to solve the next three problems.

9. Calculate the power dissipated in a 10 Ω resistor when the voltage across it is 12 V.

10. Calculate the power dissipated in a 50 Ω resistor when the voltage across it is 10 V.

11. Calculate the voltage across a 100 Ω resistor if the energy dissipated in it is 16 Joules every second.

Power gain

12. What is the power gain of an amplifier if the input power is 2 W and the output power is 18 W?

13. What is the power gain of an amplifier if the input power is 20 mW and the output power is 1 W?

14. What is the power gain of an amplifier if the input power is 100 mW and the output power is 5 W?

15. The power gain of an amplifier is 20. Calculate the output power if the input power is 2·5 W.

16. The power gain of an amplifier is 60. Calculate the input power if the output power is 15 W.

DISTANCE, SPEED AND TIME

Average Speed

1. A model car travels at a constant speed of 6 m/s.
   How far will it travel in 4 s?

2. A rugby player runs at a constant speed of 4·5 m/s. How far will he run in 5 s?

3. How long does it take a car travelling at 20 m/s to cover a mile (1600 m)?

4. How long does it take a lorry travelling at 14 m/s to cover 2814 m?

5. A sprinter's best time for 200 m is 25 s.
   Assuming she maintained a constant speed throughout the race, calculate her
   average speed.

6. A train covers the 640km from Glasgow to London in 6 hours. Calculate the average speed
   of the train in kilometers per hour.

7. A bus travelling at constant speed covers 1 km in 1 minute 40 s. Find the speed of the bus
   in metres per second.

8. A man pedals a bicycle at a constant speed of 6 m/s.
   How far would he cycle in:

   (a) 2 min?

   (b) 5 min 42 s?

9. A dog walks north at 4 m/s for 1 minute and then turns
   south and walks back the way he came at 3 m/s for 1 min.

   (a) How far did the dog walk altogether?

   (b) How far is he from where he started?

10. A man walks at 4 km/h for 1 hour. He then speeds up to
    6 km/h for another hour.

    (a) How far did he walk in the two hours?

    (b) What was his average speed for the whole journey?

11. A car travels for two hours at 30 km/h, then for three hours at 40 km/h.
    What is the average speed for the complete journey?

12. A motor cycle takes 6 hours to cover 180 km and then speeds up to 40 km/h for a further 2 hours.
    What is the average speed for the whole journey?

13. An athlete ran the 1500 metres in 3 minutes 40 s.
    Assuming he kept the same pace throughout the race, how fast was he running?

14. The Sun is 93 000 000 miles from the Earth.
    How long will it take a beam of light from the Sun to reach Earth?
    (Speed of light = 3×10^8 m/s; take 1 mile = 1600 metres.)

15. A boy shouts up a canyon and 3 s later hears the echo of the sound wave.
    If the velocity of the sound is 340 m/s, how far is he from the canyon wall?

Instantaneous Speed

1. A trolley with a 3 cm card mounted on top travels at constant velocity along a track.
    The card cuts a beam of light which is connected to a timer.
    If the timer reading indicates that the card took 0·1 s to pass through the beam, what was the velocity of the trolley?

2. A trolley with a 4 cm card mounted on top travels at constant velocity along a track.
    The card cuts a beam of light which is connected to a timer. The experiment is repeated for various speeds of the trolley and the times taken for the card to pass through the beam are listed below.
    Calculate the speed of the trolley which corresponds to each time:

    (a)   0·5 s,   *(b)*   0·05 s,

    (c)   0·04 s,   *(d)*   0·01 s.

    Answers should be in m/s.

    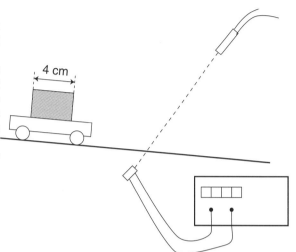

3. Andrew's electric train races into the tunnel he has just finished building. Ross, his big brother, decides to measure the speed of the train just as it enters the tunnel.

    (a)   Copy the diagram above, adding any apparatus Ross would need to measure the speed of the train.

    (b)   What measurements would Ross make?

    (c)   How could he use these measurements to calculate the speed?

4. The diameter of a football (20 cm) cuts a light beam for 0·25 s.

    (a)   How fast was the football travelling?

    (b)   The football was kicked through the light beam a second time, only this time it was faster. Predict the time on the timer.

    (c)   Could a hand-held stopwatch be used instead of the electronic timer?

5. Could a light beam be used to measure the instantaneous speed of a rugby ball? Explain.

Acceleration 1

1. A car, initially at rest, accelerates constantly at 4 m/s^2 along a level road.
    How fast will it be travelling after:

    (a)   2 s,

    (b)   3 s,

    (c)   5 s,

    (d)   5·5 s?

2. The acceleration of gravity is 10 m/s^2 . A stone is dropped from the top of a cliff.
    How fast will it be travelling after:
    (a)   1 s,
    (b)   2 s,
    (c)   3 s,
    (d)   3·5 s?

3. A motorcycle accelerates constantly
    from 20 m/s to 35 m/s in 3 s.
    Calculate the acceleration.

4. A car accelerates constantly from 8 m/s to 16 m/s in 4 s. Calculate the acceleration.

5. A bus accelerates constantly from 6 m/s to 16 m/s in 20 s. Calculate the acceleration.

6. A Vauxhall Cavalier accelerates constantly from rest to 27 m/s in 12·0 s. Calculate the acceleration.

7. A BMW 325i accelerates constantly from rest to 27 m/s in 7·6 s. Calculate the acceleration.

8. A sports car accelerates constantly from rest to 27 m/s in 5·8 s. Calculate the acceleration.

9. A car travelling at 24 m/s crashes into a wall and comes to rest in 0·15 s.
Calculate the deceleration of the car.

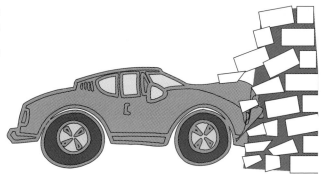

10. Two men push a heavy car and cause it to accelerate constantly from rest to 4 m/s in 8 s.

(a) Calculate the acceleration of the car.

(b) How long did it take the car to reach a speed of 3 m/s?

11. A trolley moving down an inclined plane accelerates constantly from 1·6 cm/s to 2·4 cm/s in 2 s.

(a) What is the acceleration of the trolley?

(b) How fast was the trolley moving after 1 s?

12. A cyclist freewheeling down a hill accelerates constantly from 4 m/s to 5·5 m/s in 6 s.

(a) What is the acceleration of the cyclist?

(b) Assuming he maintains this acceleration, how fast will he be travelling 9 s after the start?

(c) How long would it take the cyclist to reach a speed of 10·5 m/s after the start?

13. A ball bearing is placed at point A and rolls down a slope to point B. Given that the acceleration is constant,

(a) find the average speed between A and B.

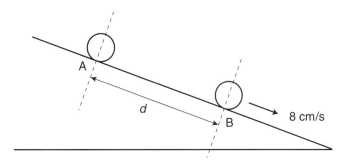

(b) If the ball bearing takes 3 s to travel from A to B, what is the length of *d* in the diagram?

(c) Calculate the acceleration of the ball bearing.

14. A lorry driver brakes and decelerates at a constant rate from 12 m/s to rest in 4 s.
  (a) Calculate the deceleration.
  (b) What was the average speed during the braking?
  (c) What was the braking distance of the lorry in this particular case?

15. A boy rolls a marble down a slope in the pavement. Two seconds after leaving his hand, the marble has a velocity of 9 cm/s.
  If the marble accelerates constantly at 2 cm/s^2 , at what velocity did it leave the boy's hand?

16. A race over 100 m is organised between an Olympic athlete and a sports car. The athlete runs the 100 m in 10 s. The car, starting from rest, accelerates constantly at 2·2 m/s^2.
  Where is the car when the athlete crosses the line?

Acceleration 2 — Light Gates

1. A trolley with a 10 cm card mounted on it is released from rest and rolls down an incline. The card cuts a light beam 3 s later (see stopwatch) and registers a time of 0·20 s on the electronic timer.
  (a) Calculate the velocity of the trolley as it passes through the light beam.
  (b) Hence calculate the acceleration of the trolley.

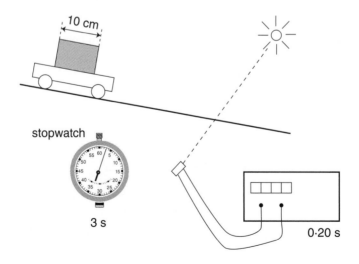

2. A trolley with a 10 cm card mounted on it is released from rest and rolls down an incline. The card cuts two light beams, each of which is connected to a separate electronic timer. A stopwatch measures the time taken for the trolley to travel from X to Y.

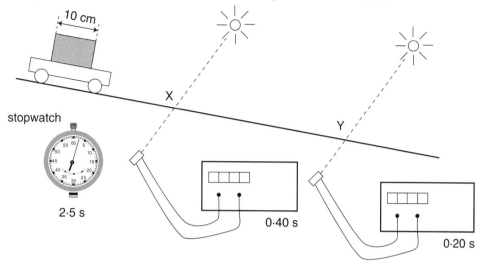

The experimental results are shown in the diagram.

(a)   Calculate the velocity at X.

(b)   Calculate the velocity at Y.

(c)   Calculate the acceleration between X and Y.

3. A trolley with a 4 cm card mounted on it rolls down an incline and cuts two light beams at X and Y. A stopwatch measures the time between X and Y.

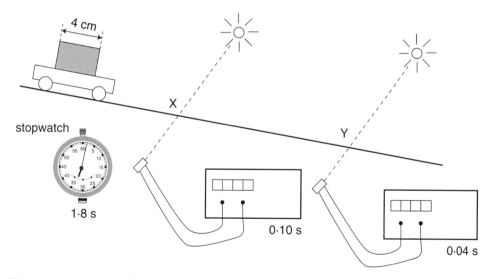

The experimental results are shown in the diagram.

(a) Calculate the velocity at X.

(b) Calculate the velocity at Y.

(c) Calculate the acceleration between X and Y.

4.   A vehicle with a 3 cm card mounted on it accelerates along a linear air track and cuts two light beams at X and Y. A third electronic timer measures the time for the vehicle to travel from X to Y.

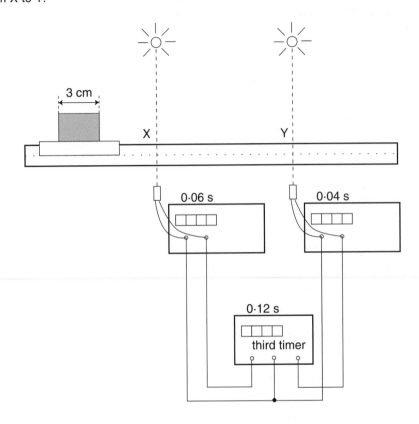

The experimental results are shown in the diagram.

(a)   Calculate the velocity at X.

(b)   Calculate the velocity at Y.

(c)   Calculate the acceleration between X and Y.

(d)   Could the third timer be replaced with a manual stopwatch? Explain.

Speed / Time Graphs

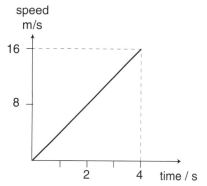

1. A car accelerates constantly from rest to 16 m/s in 4 s (as shown in the graph). Calculate the acceleration.

2. A car accelerates constantly from rest to 15 m/s in 3 s.

   (a) Draw a speed / time graph of the motion.

   (b) Calculate the acceleration.

3. A trolley accelerates constantly from rest to 4 m/s in 10 s.

   (a) Draw a speed / time graph of the motion.

   (b) Calculate the acceleration.

4. A motorcycle accelerates constantly from rest to 30 m/s in 6 s.

   (a) Draw a speed / time graph of the motion.

   (b) Calculate the acceleration.

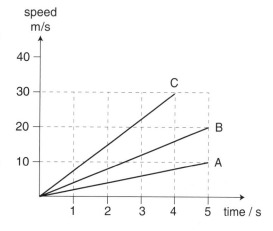

5. Three cars, A, B and C, accelerate constantly as shown in the graph.

   (a) FInd the acceleration of A.

   (b) Find the acceleration of B.

   (c) Find the acceleration of C.

   (d) Which gradient is the steepest?

   (e) Copy and complete:

   The .... the gradient, the .... the acceleration.

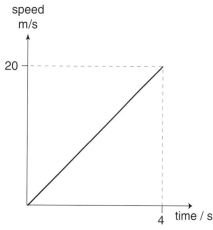

6. A vehicle accelerates as shown in the graph. Calculate:

   (a) the total distance gone;

   (b) the average speed.

7. Study the graph closely.
Calculate:

(a) the total distance gone in 6 s;

(b) the average speed.

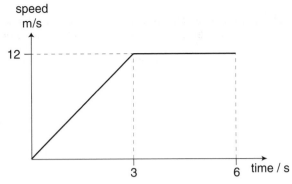

8. A motorcycle accelerates from 4 m/s to 16 m/s in 3 s and then travels at a constant speed for 3 s.
Calculate:

(a) the total distance gone in 6 s;

(b) the average speed.

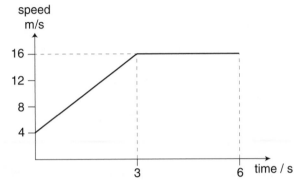

9. A car accelerates for 4 s, travels at a constant speed for 4 s and decelerates to rest in 2 s as shown in the graph.
Calculate:

(a) the total distance gone;

(b) the average speed.

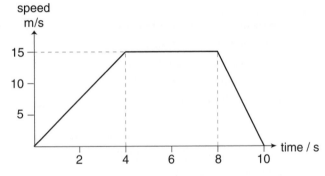

10. A vehicle on a test track accelerates twice for 4 s with a 3 s interval between (see graph).
Calculate:

(a) the total distance gone;   (b) the average speed;   (c) each acceleration.

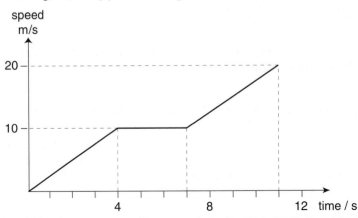

11. A car accelerates constantly from rest to 20 m/s in 4 s, travels at constant speed for another 4 s and then decelerates to rest in 2 s (see graph).

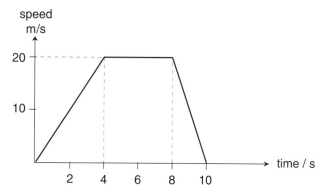

(a) Calculate the acceleration in the first 4 s.

(b) Calculate the acceleration in the last 2 s.

(c) FInd the total distance gone.

(d) What is the average speed?

Instructions for questions 12, 13 and 14

Draw a speed / time graph of the motion and use it to find:

(a) the acceleration at the start;

(b) the acceleration at the end;

(c) the total distance gone;

(d) the average speed.

12. A Ford Escort accelerates from rest to 12 m/s in 4 s. It travels at constant speed for 6 s and then decelerates to rest in a further 2 s.

13. A motorcycle accelerates from 5 m/s to 10 m/s in 2 s. It then maintains this steady speed for 4 s. Next it accelerates at 5 m/s^2 for 4 s.

14. A hot air balloon accelerates upwards from rest to 4 m/s in 30 s. The balloonist increases the acceleration so that the speed doubles over the next 15 s.

15. A very clever Volvo advert boasted about its safety. It said the car could be brought to rest from 45 m/s in only 12 s.

(a) Draw a speed / time graph of the motion and use it to find the braking distance of the Volvo.

(b) State any assumptions made.

SECTION 2

FORCES AND FRICTION

1. John steps on the scales and the reading is 70 kg. John says his weight is 70 kg. John's teacher corrects him, "Your mass is 70 kg but your weight is the gravitational force acting on your mass".
Calculate John's weight.

2. Given the mass of the following objects, calculate the weight of each:
   (a) 1 kg bag of sugar;
   (b) 5 kg bag of potatoes;
   (c) 52 kg girl;
   (d) 1200 kg car;
   (e) 100 g bar of chocolate.

3. The gravitational field strength of the earth is 10 N/kg.
   What is the force acting on the following masses?
   (a) 4 kg,
   (b) 11 kg,
   (c) 18 kg,
   (d)) 21·2 kg.

4. On the Moon the gravitational field strength is only $\frac{1}{6}$ of that on Earth.
   (a) What size is the gravitational field strength on the Moon?
   (b) How much faster or slower will a 20 kg mass fall on the Earth compared with the Moon?

5. An astronaut has a mass of 80 kg.
   The gravitational field strength on the Earth = 10 N/kg.
   The gravitational field strength on Mars = 3.8 N/kg.
   (a) Calculate his weight on Earth.
   (b) Calculate his weight on Mars.
   (c) Under what circumstances could the astronaut have no weight? Would he also have no mass?

6. In a linear air track, air is blown through a series of small holes to lift a vehicle clear of the track. This is to cut down friction.
   Give two other examples of cutting down friction which you could demonstrate in the laboratory.

7. Skydiver B jumps out of a plane 2 seconds after skydiver A. They want to link up before opening their parachutes.
   (a) What does A have to do?
   (b) What does B have to do?

8. *(a)* How could a swimmer make her body more streamlined for a race?
   (b) Speed skaters wear all-in-one body suits for racing. What advantages do these suits give the skaters?

9. This list gives the C_D measure of how streamlined a car is.

   Which car is the
   (a) most streamlined,
   (b) least streamlined?

Car	C_D
Volvo 740	0·40
Ford Escort	0·36
Austin Mini	0·48
Audi 100	0·30

10. Racing cars are very streamlined in order to achieve high speeds. Even so, any racing car will have a maximum speed.
    Explain in terms of forces why it cannot exceed this maximum speed.

NEWTON'S FIRST LAW

1. Write down Newton's first law.

2. In outer space, far enough away from any planets, things appear to be "weightless".
   Two astronauts inside their spaceship have an argument and one picks up a hammer and hits the other one over the head.
   (a) Will the astronaut feel the hammer even though it is weightless?
   (b) Explain your answer in terms of forces.

3. At carnivals, a popular game uses an "air table" to cut down friction and the two contestants hit the round flat disc.
   (a) Why is the air so important?
   (b) What would happen if the game were played without air?

4. When a bus brakes sharply, any passengers who are standing inside appear to be thrown towards the front of the bus.
   Use Newton`s first law to explain why this happens.

5. A soldier accelerates earthwards at 10 m/s/s before opening his parachute. When the parachute is open, he glides down at constant velocity.
   (a) How does the parachute create force?
   (b) Draw a diagram showing the forces acting after the parachute has been opened.

NEWTON'S SECOND LAW

1. What unbalanced force is required to accelerate a 2 kg ball at 6 m/s^2?

2. What unbalanced force is required to accelerate a 1200 kg car at 3 m/s^2?

3. What is the acceleration of a 4 kg mass when an unbalanced force of 48 N acts on it?

4. What is the acceleration of a 6 kg mass when an unbalanced force of 36 N acts on it?

5. An unbalanced force of 20 N gives a trolley a constant acceleration of 5 m/s^2. What is the mass of the trolley?

6. An unbalanced force of 160 N acting on a mass produces a constant acceleration of 10 m/s^2.
    (a) Calculate the mass.
    (b) Suggest a physical situation to explain what is happening to the mass.

7. Copy the final column from the table below and use Newton's second law to find the unknown.

	Force	Mass	Acceleration	Answer
(a)	?	101 kg	9 m/s^2	
(b)	18 000 N	?	1·2 m/s^2	
(c)	160 N	25 kg	?	
(d)	100 N	?	0·25 m/s^2	
(e)	?	2×10^3 kg	3·5 m/s^2	

8. A trolley is pulled with a 16 N force. The force of friction acts against this force and has a magnitude of 4 N.
    If the mass of the trolley is 1·5 kg, what is the acceleration?

9. An unbalanced force of 200 N acts on a 25 kg mass.
    (a) What is the acceleration of the mass?
    (b) What is the velocity of the mass after 3 s?

10. Forces act on a trolley, mass 2 kg, initially at rest as shown in the diagram.

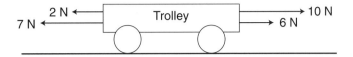

Find:

(a) the resultant force acting on the trolley;

(b) the acceleration of the trolley;

(c) the direction that the trolley moves in;

(d) the velocity of the trolley after 3 s.

11. Forces act on a 1·5 kg mass as shown.

Find:

(a) the resultant force acting on the mass;

(b) the acceleration of the mass;

(c) the velocity of the mass after 3·5 s.

12. A toy car accelerates constantly from 12 m/s to 20 m/s in 2 s. The mass of the toy car is 0·9 kg.

(a) Calculate the acceleration.

(b) What unbalanced force is required to cause this acceleration?

13. A vehicle accelerates constantly from 5 m/s to 20 m/s in 3 s under the action of an unbalanced force of 75 N.

(a) Calculate the acceleration.

(b) What is the mass of the vehicle?

14. A car accelerates from 12 m/s to 30 m/s in 6 s. The mass of the car is 1240 kg (including driver).

(a) What unbalanced force is required to cause this acceleration?

(b) The force produced by the car engine is greater than the answer to part *(a)*. Why **must** it be?

15. The graph shows part of the journey of a 1500 kg car (including driver).

    (a) Calculate the acceleration during the first 5 s.

    (b) What unbalanced force would be required to produce this acceleration?

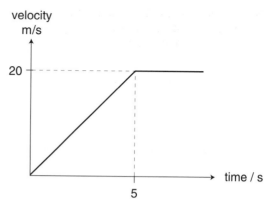

16. A 1800 kg car (including driver) accelerates from rest to 30 m/s in 6 s. It travels at this steady speed for 4 s and then decelerates to rest in another 4 s.
Draw a speed / time graph of the journey and find:

    (a) the acceleration at the start of the journey;

    (b) the unbalanced force required to cause this acceleration;

    (c) the acceleration at the end of the journey;

    (d) the unbalanced force required to cause this acceleration.

17. A 250 kg cart (including driver) accelerates from 15 m/s to 19 m/s in 8 s and then travels at constant speed for 4 s.
Draw a speed / time graph of the journey and find:

    (a) the acceleration at the start;

    (b) the unbalanced force required to cause this acceleration;

    (c) the resultant force acting during the last 4 s.

18. A golfer hits a 0·2 kg golf ball and accelerates it to 16 m/s.

golf ball

If the time of contact between the golf club and the golf ball is 4×10^{-3} s, what is the average force acting on the ball?
(Hint: first find the acceleration of the golf ball.)

19. A man exerts a 270 N force on a rope which runs over a pulley to a 9 kg mass as shown in the diagram.
Calculate:

(a) the force acting down on the mass due to gravity;

(b) the resultant force acting on the 9 kg mass;

(c) the acceleration of the mass.

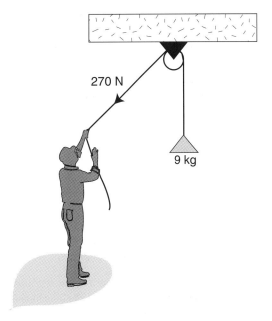

270 N

9 kg

20. A boy exerts a 60 N force on a 3 kg mass which is hanging over the edge of a cliff. What is the acceleration of the mass?

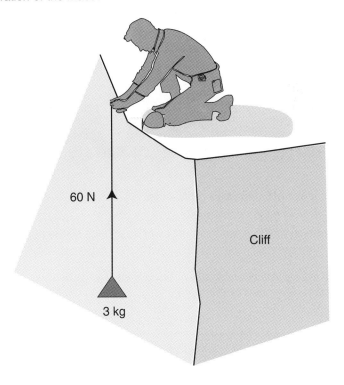

60 N

Cliff

3 kg

SECTION 3

WORK DONE AND POWER

1. A man drags a mass 200 m using a 50 N force.
   How much work has he done?

2. A dog pulls a 5 kg sledge 20 m.
   What is the work done by the dog if it exerts a 60 N force?

3. A man used up 1200 joules (J) by pulling a trolley 60 m.
   What constant force did the man exert on the trolley?

4. A girl used up 3850 J of energy when she pushed her bike 35 m along a level road.
   Calculate the constant force she exerted on the bike.

5. A boy pushes a cart with a 120 N force.
   How far does he have to push to use up 600 J of energy?

6. A locomotive exerts a force of 10 000 N on a loaded wagon.
   If the energy expended is 5 million joules, how far has the wagon moved?

7. A pupil pushes a trolley 6 m using a 10 N force.
   (a) What is the work done by the pupil?
   (b) If this operation took 5 s, what is the power developed by the pupil?

8. A man pushes a 5 kg wheelbarrow 100 m using a 40 N force in 32 s.
   What is the power developed by the man?

9. A man pulls a sledge with 160 N force.
   If the sledge moves at a steady speed of 12 m/s, what is the power developed by the man?

10. A woman exerting 120 N force pushes a pram at a steady speed of 1·4 m/s.
    What is the power developed by the woman?

11. A girl uses a spring balance to lift a 1 kg mass to a height of 1 m above the laboratory floor. The spring balance reads 10 N.

   (a) Calculate the work done by the girl.

   (b) Calculate the increase in potential energy of the mass.

12. In an experiment to calculate the power developed by a man, he runs up a flight of stairs as fast as he can.
   Given the fact that the man took 5.0 seconds to run up the stairs, use the information in the diagram to calculate his power.

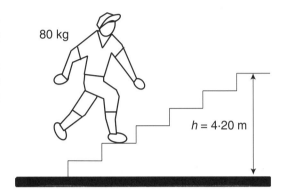

13. A 6 kg mass is pulled up an incline of 1 in 3 by a 60 N force.

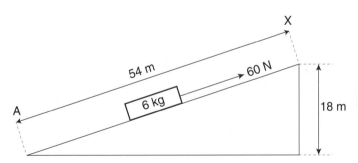

   (a) What is the work done in moving the mass from A to X?

   (b) How much potential energy does the mass have at point X?

14. A 30 kg mass is pulled up an incline of 1 in 10 by an applied force of 150 N.

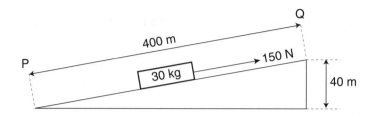

(a) What is the work done in moving the mass from P to Q?

(b) How much potential energy does the mass have at point Q?

15. A 40 kg mass is pulled up an inclined plane by a 200 N force.

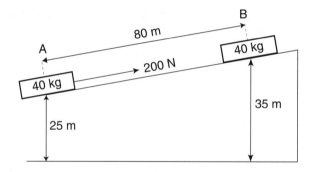

(a) What is the increase in potential energy of the mass between A and B?

(b) What is the work done in pulling the mass up the incline from A to B?

(c) Account for the difference in the answers to parts (a) and (b).

POTENTIAL AND KINETIC ENERGY

1. What is the potential energy of a 10 kg mass 25 metres above the ground?

2. A 3 kg mass is 20 m above the ground. How much potential energy does it have?

3. How high must you raise a 25 kg mass before it has a potential energy of 8500 J?

4. How high must you raise a 2 kg mass before it has a potential energy of 10 J?

5. A mass has a potential energy of 1000 J when it is 40 m above ground level. What is the mass?

6. A mass has a potential energy of 20 J when it is 50 cm above ground level. What is the mass?

7. A mass has a potential energy of 800 J when it is 16 m above the ground. How much potential energy does it have when it is:

   (a) 8 m above the ground;

   (b) 12 m above the ground;

   (c) 4 m above the ground;

   (d) 15 m above the ground?

   What is the mass?

8. What is the kinetic energy of a 70 kg footballer running at 5 m/s?

9. What is the kinetic energy of a 90 kg rugby player running at 4 m/s?

10. An unknown mass has a kinetic energy of 400 J when it is travelling with a velocity of 40 m/s. What is the mass?

11. A car has a kinetic energy of 200 000 J when it is travelling at 20 m/s. What is the mass of the car?

12. A model racer (mass 10 kg) moves along a circuit at a constant velocity. If it has a kinetic energy of 3125 J, how fast is it travelling?

13. A lorry (mass 3000 kg) is moving at constant velocity. If it has a kinetic energy of 150 000 J, how fast is it travelling?

14. A 60 kg athlete can run the mile (1600 m) in exactly 4 minutes. Assuming he maintains a constant velocity, find his kinetic energy during the race.

15. A pendulum swings as shown in the diagram.

(a) At what point(s) does the pendulum have maximum kinetic energy?

(b) At what point(s) does the pendulum have maximum potential energy?

(c) Eventually the pendulum comes to a halt. Where has the energy gone?

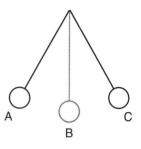

16. A pendulum swings as shown in the diagram. Points A and C are the extremities of the swing of the pendulum. The mass of the bob is 0·5 kg.

Find:

(a) the maximum potential energy of the bob;

(b) the maximum kinetic energy of the bob;

(c) the top speed of the bob.

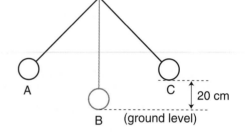

17. A pendulum swings from a point of maximum potential energy (X) to the point of minimum potential energy (Y) as shown in the diagram. The mass of the bob is I kg.
How fast is the bob moving at point Y?

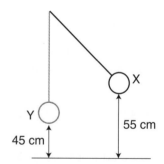

18. The maximum velocity of a pendulum bob is 4 m/s. If the mass of the bob is 0·6 kg, find the maximum potential energy of the pendulum.

19. A 2 kg mass is 20 m above the ground. It falls and all the potential energy is converted into kinetic energy. What is the velocity of the mass just before it hits the ground?

20. A 6 kg mass is 20 m above the ground. It falls and all the potential energy is converted into kinetic energy. What is the velocity of the mass just before it hits the ground?

21. By careful examination of the answers to questions 19 and 20, form a conclusion about the mass.

22. A 0·6 kg stone is thrown upwards with a velocity of 30 m/s.

(a) How high will the stone go?

(b) What will be the velocity of the stone when it hits the ground (neglect air resistance)?

23. An unbalanced force of 60 N pulls a mass of 4 kg which is initially at rest.

(a) What is the acceleration?

(b) What is the speed after 3 s?

(c) What is the kinetic energy of the mass at this speed?

24. An unbalanced force of 120 N acts on a 30 kg mass initially at rest.

(a) What is the acceleration?

(b) What is the velocity after 5 s and what is the kinetic energy of the mass at this velocity?

(c) An identical 30 kg mass is a certain height above the ground. If the potential energy of this mass is the same as the kinetic energy of the previous mass, what is the height above the ground?

25. *(a)* John throws a ball down against the road and it bounces higher than the position at which it left his hand (see diagram). John sees that the ball has bounced higher and therefore has more potential energy than when it left his hand. He concludes that the ground gave the ball energy. Explain whether you think John was right or wrong.

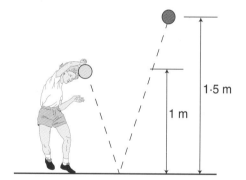

(b) A gun fires a shell as shown in the diagram. The gunner who fired the gun notes that the shell gains potential energy between Y and X. His gunnery officer told him that the horizontal velocity of the shell does not change. He is therefore puzzled how the shell gained energy.

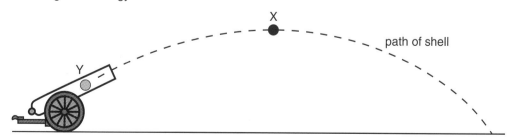

Write a detailed explanation of what is happening to the shell in terms of potential and kinetic energy.

SUPPLY AND DEMAND

1. Which of the following are fossil fuels:

   coal,   wind,   oil,   nuclear,   solar?

2. Suggest one way of conserving energy in a house.

3. The government are encouraging people to car-share to and from work.
   What has this to do with energy conservation?

4. A factory has one hundred 100 W bulbs. The factory manager wants to convert to 100 W
   fluorescent tubes because they are more efficient. He argues that his electricity bill will go
   down but his foreman thinks the electricity bill will not change.
   Who is right — and why?

5. Sources of energy can be classified into renewable and non-renewable.

Renewable	Non-renewable

   Copy the table above and enter the following sources of energy in the correct column:
       coal,   oil,   solar,   wind,   nuclear,   hydroelectric,   gas.

6. A satellite has two large arms which are covered in solar cells.

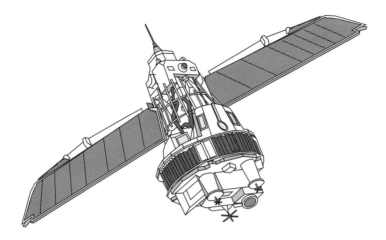

(a) What is the energy conversion in a solar cell?

(b) Complete the sentence:
    The larger the surface area of the solar cells, the .... electrical energy
    is produced.

(c) The angle of the arms in space is very important. Explain.

7. A model of a solar panel has water flowing through a pipe which is heated constantly by a heat lamp.

(a) What happens to the temperature of the water as it flows through the pipe?

(b) Why is the pipe bent inside the solar panel?

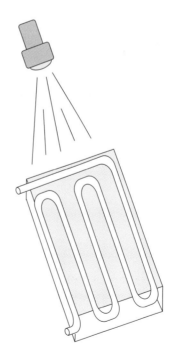

8. A motorcycle engine has little "fins" sticking out to let air pass between them as the motorcycle moves at speed.

Why is the engine designed this way?

9. State a disadvantage of each of the following renewable energy sources:

    (a) solar,

    (b) wind,

    (c) geothermal.

10. State an advantage of each of the following renewable energy sources:

    (a) solar,

    (b) wind,

    (c) waves.

11. A wind generator produces 3000 kW of electrical power. How much energy (kWh) will it produce in

    (a) 1 hour,

    (b) 1 day?

12. A factory makes solar panels measuring 2 m × 2 m.
    In the UK, each 1 m^2 is struck by 200 J of energy per second.
    A woman has 5 panels on her roof.

    (a) Calculate the power of 1 panel.

    (b) Calculate the power of all 5 panels.

    (c) The woman would not receive this power inside her house. Why not?

SECTION 2

GENERATION OF ELECTRICITY

1. In an oil-fired power station, the oil is burned in the furnace and heats water, turning it into steam.
   (a) What is the energy change in the furnace?
   (b) The steam is piped to a steam turbine which spins and turns a generator. What is the energy change in the generator?

2. In a hydroelectric power station, water runs down a mountain and spins a water turbine which turns a generator.
   (a) High up the mountain, what type of energy does the water have?
   (b) What is the energy change as the water runs down the mountain?
   (c) What is the energy change in the generator?

3. Study this list.
   Oil-fired power station.
   Coal-fired power station.
   Hydroelectric power station.
   Nuclear power station.
   (a) Which of the above has / have a boiler?
   (b) Which of the above has / have a heat exchanger?

4. Near Dalmally, in Scotland, there is a pumped storage power station.
   (a) During the day water flows down the mountain. How does this produce electricity?
   (b) At night, electricity is used to pump water back up the mountain to fill a reservoir. Why is this done at night?
   (c) What is the advantage of pumping water back up the mountain?

5. 1 tonne of coal produces $2 \cdot 8 \times 10^{10}$ J
   1 kg of uranium produces 9×10^{16} J
   1 tonne = 1000 kg

   (a) How much energy is produced from 1 kg of coal?

   (b) Calculate the ratio of $\dfrac{\text{energy from 1 kg of uranium}}{\text{energy from 1 kg of coal}}$.

6. Starting with one neutron striking a uranium nucleus to produce two fission fragments and three neutrons, draw a diagram to explain a chain reaction.

7.   A 6 kg mass is pulled up an incline of 1 in 3 by a 60 N force.

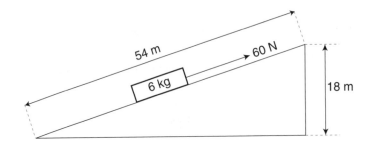

54 m   60 N

6 kg

18 m

    (a)   Calculate the energy input.

    (b)   Calculate the energy output.

    (c)   Calculate the efficiency of the machine.

8.   An electric motor lifts a 1·5 kg mass 2 m vertically in 9 s.
    The electric motor draws a current of 0·75 A from the 12 V supply.

    (a)   Calculate the electrical energy supplied in 9 s.

    (b)   Calculate the potential energy gained by the mass in this time.

    (c)   Calculate the efficiency of the machine.

9.   By exerting a force of 600 N through a distance of 20 m, a man lifts a 40 kg mass 20 m.

    (a)   What is the work done by the man?

    (b)   What is the potential energy gained by the mass?

    (c)   Calculate the efficiency of the machine.

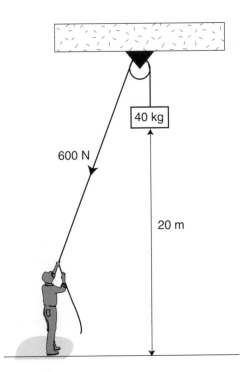

40 kg

600 N

20 m

10. By exerting a 200 N force through 16 m, a man uses a block and tackle to lift a 60 kg mass 4 m.

   (a) What is the work done by the man?

   (b) What is the potential energy gained by the mass?

   (c) Calculate the efficiency of the machine.

   (d) If it took the man 10 s to raise the mass, what was the power developed by his body?

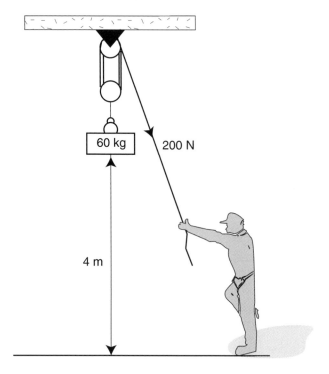

SECTION 3

ELECTROMAGNETIC INDUCTION AND THE TRANSFORMER

1. A magnet is moved into a coil of wire which is attached to a centre zero galvanometer as shown.

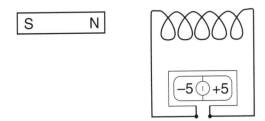

Moving the north pole in makes the galvanometer reading change from zero to +5 on the scale.

(a) What happens to the reading when the magnet stops inside the coil?

(b) What happens to the reading when the magnet is moved out again (at the same rate as before)?

(c) What happens to the reading when the magnet stops outside the coil?

(d) What difference does it make to the current reading if the magnet is moved **slowly** or **quickly** into the coil?

2. (a) The magnet in question 1 is replaced with a stronger magnet. What difference does this make to the induced current when the magnet is pushed into the coil?

(b) The coil in question 1 is replaced with a coil with more turns. What difference does this make to the induced current when the original magnet is pushed into the coil?

3. (a) A wire linked to a galvanometer is moved up and down between two poles of a horseshoe magnet as shown in the diagram.

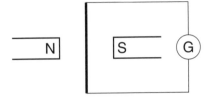

Does the galvanometer show a deflection when the wire is moving?

(b) The wire is now turned through 90° and moved up and down again between the two pole pieces as shown in the diagram.

Does the galvanometer show a deflection when the wire is moving this time?
Explain both these observations making appropriate reference to lines of force.

4. The diagram shows the main parts of an a.c. generator. Copy the diagram and mark in the:

Input,
Output,
Rotor,
Stator Coil.

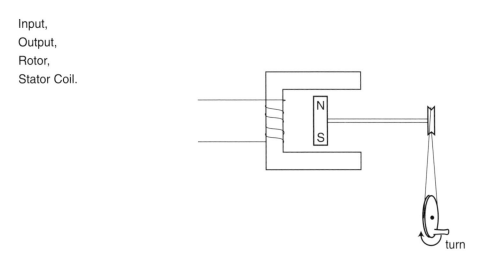

5. Making reference to the diagram in question 4, **explain** how electricity is produced.

6. Outline two main differences between a full-size generator and the simple generator shown in question 4.

7. The circuit shows an a.c. source connected to a coil which is wound round one arm of a metal frame. The other arm of the metal frame has a separate coil wound round it and a bulb connected to the coil.

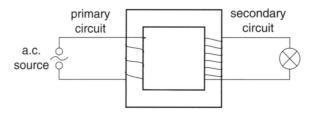

A changing current in the primary circuit produces a changing magnetic field in the primary coil.

(a) How does this affect the secondary coil?

(b) This in turn causes a current to flow through the bulb. Is the current a.c. or d.c.?

(c) If the a.c. source was replaced with a d.c. source, how would this affect the bulb? Why does this happen?

8. Two coils are wound one on top of another using a wooden rod as the centre. An a.c. source is attached to one coil and a resistor and ammeter are attached to the other coil.

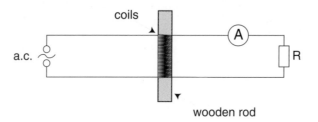

(a) Will the ammeter register a current?

(b) Given any additional apparatus you may need, outline three ways to increase the magnetic field between the two coils.

(c) If this field is increased, what will happen to the reading on the ammeter?

9. A large coil with a hollow centre is connected to a d.c. supply. A model railway wagon with a bar magnet fixed to one end sits on a track on one side of the coil.

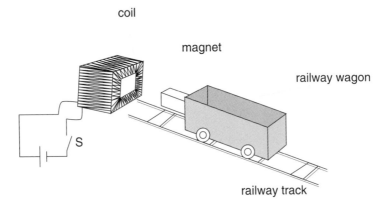

A pupil using this apparatus observes two things:

Observation 1. With switch S closed, the railway wagon is allowed to move along the track to the coil. The magnet enters the core of the coil and the wagon immediately springs backwards.

Observation 2. With switch S open, the wagon is placed so that the magnet is sitting inside the coil. When the switch is closed the wagon moves away from the coil.

Explain both these observations.

What difference would it make to each observation if the battery terminals were reversed?

10. Transformers are amongst the most efficient machines known to man. They lose energy by **copper loss**, **eddy current** and **hysteresis loss**.

Taking each of these in turn, explain what they are.

TRANSFORMERS AND VOLTAGE

Each diagram below shows a transformer with a primary coil (on the left) and a secondary coil. Three of the four quantities are given.

Voltage in primary (V_P)　　　　Number of turns in primary (N_P)
Voltage in secondary (V_S)　　　Number of turns in secondary (N_S)

Find the fourth (unknown) term.

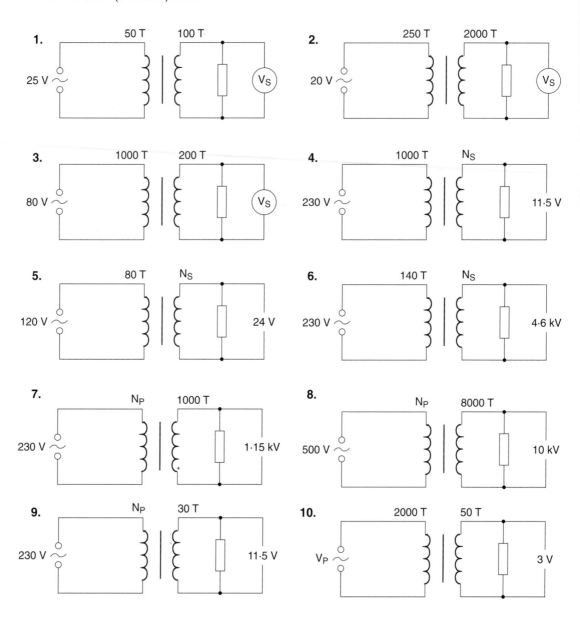

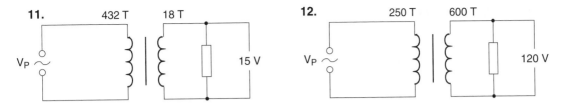

11.   432 T   18 T   **12.**   250 T   600 T

V_P 15 V V_P 120 V

TRANSFORMERS AND POWER

Assume all transformers to be 100% efficient.

1. A 125 V a.c. supply is connected to the primary circuit of a transformer with turns ratio 5 : 1.

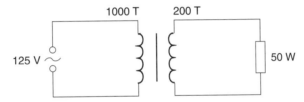

1000 T   200 T

125 V   50 W

A 50 W heater is connected across the secondary coil.

(a) What is the voltage across the heater?

(b) What is the current passing through the heater?

(c) What is the current in the primary circuit?

2. A 1 kW electric fire is operating from the secondary turns of a transformer.

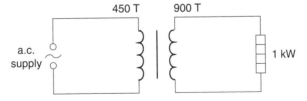

450 T   900 T

a.c.
supply   1 kW

The fire draws a current of 4 A in the secondary circuit.

(a) What is the voltage across the fire?

(b) What is the supply voltage across the primary turns?

(c) What is the current in the primary circuit?

3. An electric fire has two 1 kW bars wired in parallel and connected across the secondary turns of a transformer.

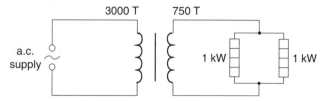

The voltage across each bar is 250 V.

(a) What is the supply voltage?

(b) What is the current in each bar of the fire?

(c) What is the current in the primary circuit?

4. Electricity is produced by a generator at a dam and carried by a power line (supported by pylons) to supply houses.
    A step-up transformer is used at the start of the power line and a step-down transformer is used at the end of the power line.

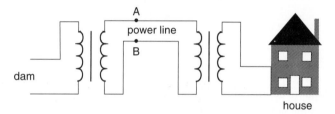

The turns ratio for the step-up transformer is 1 : 100. The turns ratio for the step-down transformer is 200 : 1. The voltage across points A and B in the power line is 50 000 V.

(a) What is the voltage of the supply coming from the dam?

(b) What is the voltage of the supply going to the house (assuming no resistance in the power line)?

(c) We prefer to "transport" electricity in a power line using **high voltage** rather than **high current**. Bearing in mind that a real power line has resistance, explain the advantages of this.

5. A transformer in a television is used to step the voltage up from 230 V to 2760 V.

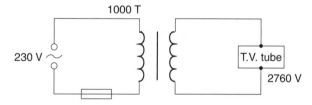

The television normally draws a 2 A current from the mains. The primary coil of the transformer has 1000 turns.

(a) How many turns are there in the secondary coil?

(b) What is the power rating of the television?

(c) Given a 3 A fuse and a 13 A fuse, which fuse would you choose for this circuit?

6. An electric heater has two identical 1 kW elements E_1 and E_2 wired in parallel and attached to the secondary coil of a transformer.

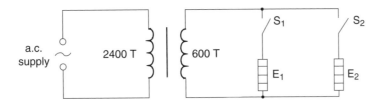

The primary coil has 2400 turns and the secondary coil has 600 turns. With S_1 open and S_2 closed, the voltage across element E_2 is 250 V and the current through it is 4 A.

(a) What is the power rating of element E_2?

(b) What is the supply voltage?

(c) What is the current in the primary circuit?

Both switches are now closed.

(d) What is the current drawn from the secondary coil?

(e) What is the current drawn from the supply?

7. A resistor is known to have a power rating of 1 W when a 1 mA current is passing through it. The resistor is attached to the secondary turns of a transformer as shown.

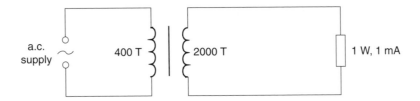

Assuming the resistor uses up 1 J of electrical energy every second, find:

(a) the voltage of the supply;

(b) the current in the primary circuit.

8. An experimental transformer is tested using a ring circuit. Three appliances can be plugged into the ring circuit, i.e. an electric fire, an electric kettle and a hair dryer. The power rating of each of these appliances is shown in the diagram.

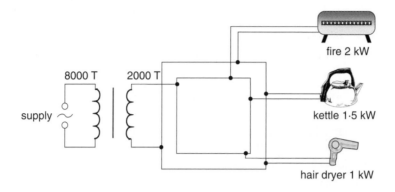

fire 2 kW

kettle 1·5 kW

hair dryer 1 kW

The voltage across the ring circuit is 250 V. The primary coil has 8000 turns and the secondary coil has 2000 turns. What is the current in the primary circuit when:

(a) only the fire is connected to the ring circuit;

(b) only the fire and kettle are connected to the ring circuit;

(c) all three appliances are connected to the ring circuit?

9. A model power line illustrates both step-up and step-down transformers as shown in the diagram.

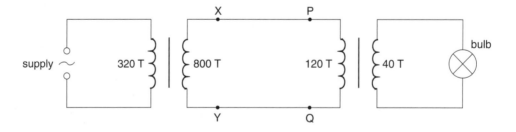

The long wires XP and YQ have resistance.
The p.d. across points X and Y is 100 V.
The p.d. across points P and Q is 90 V.
The current in the long wires XP and YQ is 0·2 A.

(a) What is the supply voltage?

(b) What is the voltage across the bulb?

(c) What is the resistance of **single** wire XP?

10. A model power line has a step-up transformer of turns ratio 1 : 8 and a step-down transformer of turns ratio 8 : 1.

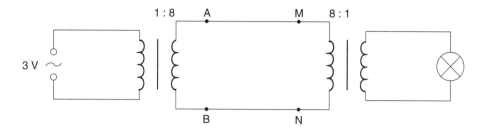

The supply voltage is 3 V.
The voltage across the bulb is 2 V.

(a) Calculate the voltage across AB.

(b) Calculate the voltage across MN.

(c) Given that the resistance of wires AM and BN is 12 Ω each, calculate the current in the wires.

(d) Calculate the power loss in the line.

SECTION 4

SPECIFIC HEAT CAPACITY

Unless otherwise stated, assume no heat loss in the following problems. The specific heat capacities shown below may be required for the problems which follow.

Water	4180 J/kg ˚C
Alcohol	2350 J/kg ˚C
Aluminium	902 J/kg ˚C
Copper	386 J/kg ˚C
Lead	128 J/kg ˚C

1. What is meant by the statement "the specific heat capacity of water is 4180 J/kg ˚C?

2. How much energy is required to give 1 kg of water a temperature rise of:
   (a) 3 ˚C,
   (b) 5 ˚C,
   (c) 2·5 ˚C?

3. How much heat is required to raise the temperature of:
   (a) 4 kg of water from 10 ˚C to 20 ˚C,
   (b) 500 g of aluminium from 100 ˚C to 500 ˚C,
   (c) 1·5 kg of copper by 100 degrees on the Celsius scale,
   (d) 50 g of lead from 50 ˚C to 450 ˚C?

4. What is the rise in temperature produced when 10 000 J are supplied to:
   (a) 2 kg of water,
   (b) 2·5 kg of aluminium,
   (c) 600 g of copper,
   (d) 1·5 kg of alcohol?

5. What mass of material is present if 20 000 J produces a rise in temperature of 20˚ Celsius in,
   (a) water;
   (b) aluminium;
   (c) copper;
   (d) alcohol?

6. *(a)* 10^6 J of energy are supplied to 10 kg of copper at 20 ˚C. What will be the final temperature of the copper?
   (b) If the copper is now left to cool and loses heat at the rate of 100 J/s, what will be the temperature after 1 min 40 s?

7. A kettle with a 500 W element contains 1·5 kg of water initially at 20 ˚C.

    (a) How long will it take to boil assuming all the heat goes into the water?

    (b) How will this compare with the actual time?

8. 300 g of water at 20 ˚C are contained in a copper can of mass 100 g. The temperature of both the water and the copper can is then raised to 40 ˚C by a 50 W immersion heater.

    (a) How much heat is absorbed by the water?

    (b) How much heat is absorbed by the copper?

    (c) How long does it take?

9. A kettle with a 1 kW element contains 1 kg of water initially at a temperature of 15 ˚C. If 80% of the heat produced by the kettle goes to heating the water:

    (a) how much heat does the water absorb in going to boiling point?

    (b) what percentage of the heat supplied by the kettle does this represent? How much heat was supplied by the kettle?

    (c) what happens to the "lost" energy?

10. In an experiment to find the specific heat capacity of copper, the apparatus shown was used.

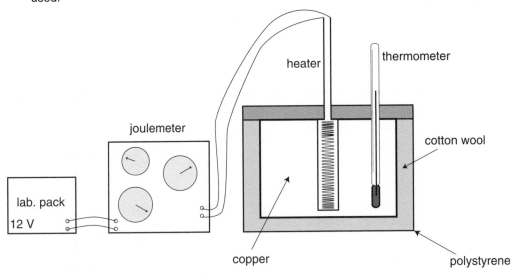

The laboratory pack supplied the energy to the heater which converted the electrical energy into heat. The joulemeter measured the energy supplied. The thermometer measured the rise in temperature of the 1 kg mass of copper.

The following experimental results were obtained:

initial reading on thermometer	=	19 °C;
final reading on thermometer	=	25 °C;
initial reading on joulemeter	=	59 500 J;
final reading on joulemeter	=	62 000 J.

(a) What was the rise in temperature of the copper?

(b) How much electrical energy was supplied?

(c) Use these results to calculate the specific heat capacity of copper.

(d) The actual specific heat of copper is 386 J / kg °C. Account for the difference between this value and the experimental value calculated in part *(c)*.

11. A heater is used to heat a 5 kg block of aluminium. The heater, operating from a 230 V supply, draws a current of 4 A.

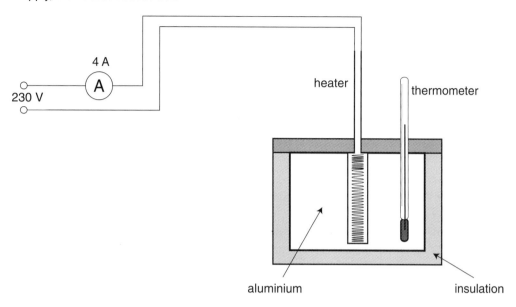

If the heater was switched on for 2 minutes:

(a) what was the electrical energy supplied to the aluminium in this time?

(b) Hence calculate the **maximum** rise in temperature possible. State any assumptions clearly.

12. A 100 W heater takes 1 minute 16 s to raise the temperature of an insulated 3 kg copper mass from 26 ˚C to 31 ˚C.

(a) What is the electrical energy supplied in this time?

(b) How much heat is absorbed by the copper?

(c) Calculate the efficiency of the system.

SPECIFIC LATENT HEAT

1. When boiling water at 100 °C is heated there is no rise in temperature. Instead of a change in temperature there is a change of state, i.e. the boiling water at 100 °C forms steam at 100 °C.

    From the scientist's point of view, heat has been put into a substance and there has been no temperature rise. Therefore this heat energy appears to have been **lost**.

    (a) Where has this heat energy gone?

    (b) What is the specific latent heat of a substance?

    (c) What is the difference between specific latent heat of fusion and specific latent heat of vaporisation of a substance?

2. Liquid Freon is pumped through a freezer. The Freon takes heat from the interior of the freezer and changes state.

    (a) What is the change in state described above?

    (b) What part of the freezer changes the Freon back to liquid?

3. A set of hair rollers loses heat slowly so that the temperature remains constant for a long time.

    How can the rollers lose heat at constant temperature?

4. The specific latent heat of fusion of ice is 3.34×10^5 J/kg. How much energy is required to change 2·6 kg of ice at 0 °C into water at the same temperature?

5. The specific latent heat of vaporisation of water is 2.26×10^6 J/kg. How much energy is required to change 2·6 kg of water at 100 °C into steam at the same temperature?

6. You are given 4 kg of ice at 0 °C and following data:

specific latent heat of fusion of ice	$= 3.34 \times 10^5$ J/kg;
specific heat capacity of water	$= 4180$ J/kg °C;
specific latent heat of vaporisation of water	$= 2.26 \times 10^6$ J/kg.

    (a) How much energy is required to melt all the ice without raising the temperature?

    (b) How much energy is required to change the 4 kg of water at 0 °C into 4 kg of boiling (100 °C) water?

    (c) How much energy is required to change all the boiling (100 °C) water into steam at the same temperature?

    (d) Hence find how much energy is required to change 4 kg of ice at 0°C into 4 kg of steam at 100 °C?

7. Using the data in question 6, calculate how much heat is required to change 1·9 kg of ice at 0 °C into 1·9 kg of steam at 100 °C.

8. In an experiment designed to calculate the specific latent heat of fusion of ice, the apparatus shown was used. The laboratory pack supplied electrical energy to the heater which converted the electrical energy into heat. This heat melted the ice (which was originally at 0 °C) and the water formed dripped into the beaker below (beaker A).

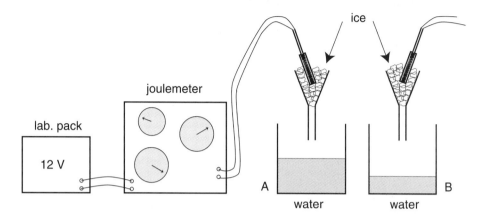

Even if no heat were supplied by the heater, some ice would melt because of heat taken in from the surrounding air. To compensate for this, an identical experimental set-up with no electrical supply measures the mass of ice melted by heat from the air (beaker B).

Some results of this experiment:

mass of water in beaker A   =   0·10 kg
mass of water in beaker B   =   0·02 kg
final reading on joulemeter   =   71 500 J
initial reading on joulemeter =   43 500 J

(a) How much ice was melted due to the action of the heater alone?

(b) How much electrical energy was supplied to the heater?

(c) Calculate the specific latent heat of fusion of ice from these results.

(d) With more accurate data, the specific latent heat of fusion of ice is found to be $3·34 \times 10^5$ J/kg. Account for the difference between this value and the value calculated in part (c).

9. A heater with a power rating of 100 W is placed in a bath of 1 kg of ice at 0 °C. For how long must the heater be on to melt half the ice? Assume no ice melts due to room temperature and assume all heat goes into the ice.
The specific latent heat of fusion of ice = $3·34 \times 10^5$ J/kg.

10. A housewife puts 0·8 kg of water, initially at a temperature of 20 ˚C, into a kettle rated at 2 kW.

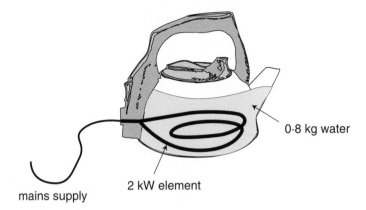

0·8 kg water

2 kW element

mains supply

Specific heat capacity of water = 4180 J/kg ˚C
Specific latent heat of vaporisation of water = $2 \cdot 26 \times 10^6$ J/kg.

Only 80% of the heat produced by the kettle goes to heating the water. The housewife leaves the kettle on and when she comes back the water in the kettle is boiling and the kitchen is full of steam. She immediately switches the kettle off and measures how much water is left. Only 0·4 kg of water is left.

(a) How much heat went into the water altogether? Include in your answer the heat required to produce the steam.

(b) What percentage of the heat supplied by the kettle does this represent? How much heat was produced in the element?

(c) For how long did the housewife leave the kettle on? (Answer to the nearest second.)

UNIT 7

SPACE PHYSICS

SECTION 1

SIGNALS FROM SPACE

THE LIGHT YEAR

1. Copy and complete the following sentences by selecting the appropriate word from the word bank.

   (a) The Earth is a ....

   (b) A moon orbits a ....

   (c) A planet orbits a ....

STAR
PLANET
MOON
UNIVERSE
GALAXY

2. How many planets are there in our solar system?

3. Is the Moon a satellite?

4. The speed of light in space is 3×10^8 m/s. How far will light travel in:

   (a) 2 seconds;

   (b) 30 seconds;

   (c) 1 minute?

5. The speed of light in space is 3×10^8 m/s. How far will light travel in:

   (a) 1 hour;

   (b) 1 day;

   (c) 1 year (365 days)?

6. How far is 1 light year?

7. The Earth is $1 \cdot 5 \times 10^8$ km from the Sun.
   Prove that light takes (about) 8 minutes to travel from the Sun to the Earth.

8. Mars is $2 \cdot 28 \times 10^8$ km from the Sun.
   How long does it take light to travel from the Sun to Mars?

9. By making reference to questions 7 and 8, calculate:

   (a) the shortest distance between the Earth and Mars;

   (b) the time it takes light to travel from Earth to Mars.

10. The nearest star is approximately $4 \cdot 3$ light years from Earth.
    How far away is this in metres?

REFRACTING TELESCOPE

1. *(a)* Copy the diagram below and label the two lenses.

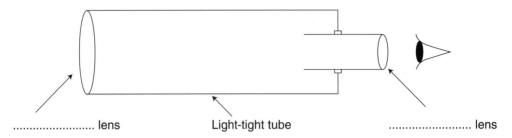

.... lens   Light-tight tube   .... lens

    (b) Does the objective lens produce an image?

2. The diameter of the objective lens in a telescope is increased.
    (a) Does the image become brighter / dimmer / no change?
    (b) Why does this happen?

3. An object (O) is placed within the focal length of a convex lens.

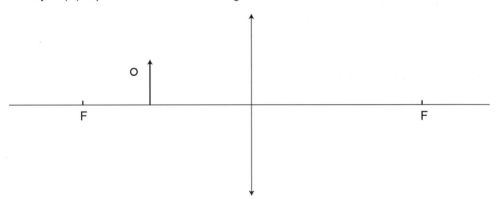

    (a) Copy and complete the diagram showing two rays coming from the object.
    (b) Use these rays to form an image.
    (c) Is the image
            real / virtual,   magnified / diminished,   erect / inverted?

4. An object 2 cm tall is placed 3 cm from a convex lens of focal length 5 cm.

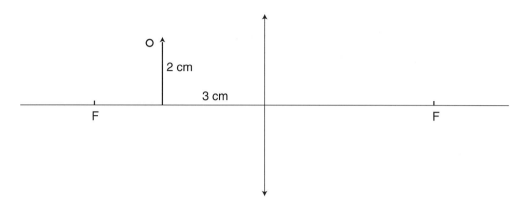

(a) Copy the diagram to scale on to graph paper.

(b) Complete the diagram to find the height of the image.

(c) How far from the lens is the image?

5. An object 2 cm tall is placed 2 cm from a convex lens of focal length 6 cm.

(a) Draw a scale diagram of the arrangement and complete the diagram to find the image.

(b) Describe the image (3 words).

SPECTROSCOPY AND THE ELECTROMAGNETIC SPECTRUM

1. White light can be split into its constituent parts using a prism.

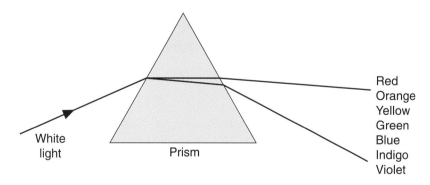

(a) In air, all the colours have the same speed / frequency / wavelength?

(b) In glass the light speeds up / slows down?

2. Copy and complete the following sentences using **longer** or **shorter**.

    (a) Red light has a .... wavelength than blue light.

    (b) Blue light has a .... wavelength than red light.

    (c) Green light has a .... wavelength than red light.

    (d) Green light has a .... wavelength than blue light.

3. What is the difference between a continuous spectrum and a line spectrum?

4. Red light from a laser strikes a prism.

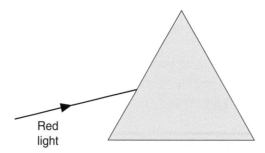

Red
light

    (a) Copy and complete the diagram showing what happens to this laser light.

    (b) The wavelength of the red light is 630 nm (630×10^{-9} m). Calculate the frequency of the red light in air.

    (c) What is the frequency of the red light in glass?

5. When light from a sodium lamp is passed through a prism it is split into a **line** spectrum.

    (a) What causes the lines?

    (b) Can any other element have the same line spectrum as sodium?

6. The line spectrum of an element (like hydrogen) is sometimes referred to as its **optical fingerprint**.

    What does this mean?

7. Light from a star is analysed by passing it through a prism to see the line spectrum.
    How can this line spectrum give us information about elements in the star?

8. The diagram below shows the line spectrum for hydrogen, helium, sodium and the spectrum from a star.

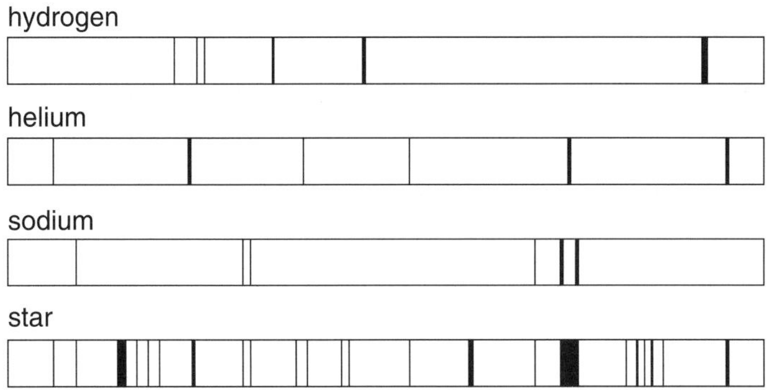

hydrogen

helium

sodium

star

(a) Is hydrogen present in the star spectrum?

(b) Is helium present in the star spectrum?

(c) Is sodium present in the star spectrum?

9. Copy and complete the table below, choosing a suitable detector for each wave.

Radiation	Detector
TV and radio	
Microwaves	
Infrared	
Visible light	
Ultraviolet	
X-rays	
Gamma rays	

10. Ultraviolet, visible light, infrared, gamma rays, X-rays, TV and radio waves, microwaves.

(a) Which of the above waves has the highest frequency?

(b) Which of the above waves has the lowest frequency?

(c) Put all the waves into order starting with the highest frequency.

SECTION 2

SPACE TRAVEL

ROCKETS

In questions 1 to 4, two trolleys are exploded apart so that they move in opposite directions. Calculate the speed v of the left-hand trolley in each case.

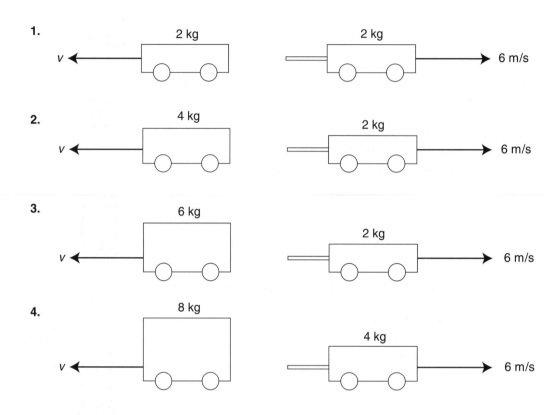

1.   2 kg   2 kg
v ←   → 6 m/s

2.   4 kg   2 kg
v ←   → 6 m/s

3.   6 kg   2 kg
v ←   → 6 m/s

4.   8 kg   4 kg
v ←   → 6 m/s

5.   A bullet of mass 100 g is fired from a 5 kg gun at 50 m/s.

v ←   → 50 m/s

5 kg   100 g

Calculate the recoil speed of the gun.

6. A model rocket of mass 50 kg is initially accelerated upwards by the thrust of the rocket engine.

(a) What is the force of gravity acting on the rocket?

(b) If the thrust force is 800 N, calculate the unbalanced force acting on the rocket.

(c) Hence calculate the acceleration of the rocket.

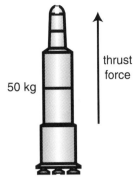

7. A rocket of mass 1200 kg is initially accelerated upwards by the thrust of the rocket engines.

(a) What is the force of gravity acting on the rocket?

(b) If the thrust force is 15 000 N, calculate the unbalanced force acting on the rocket.

(c) Hence calculate the acceleration of the rocket.

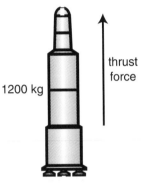

8. A rocket of mass 2000 kg is initially accelerated upwards by the thrust of the rocket engines.

(a) If the thrust force is 30 000 N, calculate the unbalanced force acting on the rocket.

(b) Hence calculate the acceleration of the rocket.

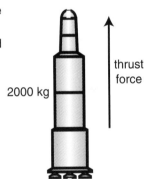

9. Initially at take-off the thrust force of a rocket is 18 000 N and the force of gravity acting on the rocket is 8000 N.

(a) Find the mass of the rocket.

(b) Hence calculate the acceleration of the rocket.

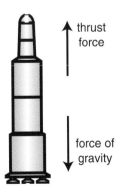

10. A rocket on the launch pad has two forces acting on it as shown in the diagram.

    (a) Calculate the initial acceleration of the rocket.

    (b) As the rocket rises, what happens to the mass?

    (c) How does this affect acceleration?

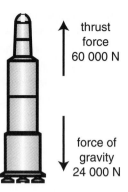

thrust
force
60 000 N

force of
gravity
24 000 N

GRAVITY AND WEIGHTLESSNESS

1. A coin and a feather are dropped together inside an evacuated tube. Both reach the bottom of the tube at the same time. Explain.

2. John's mass is 50 kg.

    (a) What is his weight on Earth?

    (b) If the gravitational field strength on the Moon is 1·6 N/kg, calculate his weight on the Moon.

3. An astronaut has a mass of 80 kg. Copy the final column of the table below and fill in his weight on each of the four planets.

Planet	Gravitational field strength / N/kg	Weight / N
Earth	10	
Mars	3·8	
Jupiter	26·4	
Saturn	11·5	

4.   A girl of mass 60 kg stands on a set of scales in a lift. When the lift is stationary the scales read 600 N.
     The lift accelerates upwards, moves at constant velocity and then decelerates to rest.
     (a)   When the lift accelerates upwards, the scales read:
               600 N;   more than 600 N;   less than 600 N.
     (b)   When the lift is moving at constant velocity, the scales read:
               600 N;   more than 600 N;   less than 600 N.
     (c)   When the lift is decelerating, the scales read:
               600 N;   more than 600 N;   less than 600 N.

5.   How will the weight of a 90 kg astronaut 10 miles above the Earth compare with his weight on the Earth?

PROJECTILE MOTION

Note: In all problems in this section, air resistance can be ignored.

1.   An electric light bulb fell from a high window. Two seconds later it hit the ground and smashed on impact.
     (a)   What was the velocity on impact?
     (b)   What was the average velocity of the bulb during the 2 s?
     (c)   How far did the bulb travel?

2.   A mass is dropped from the top of a cliff and 5 s later it hit the ground.
     (a)   With what velocity did it hit the ground?
     (b)   What was the average velocity of the mass during the 5 s?
     (c)   How far did the mass fall?

3.   A bricklayer drops a brick from his scaffolding and 2·5 s later it hits the ground.
     (a)   With what velocity does the brick strike the ground?
     (b)   What is the average velocity of the brick during its journey?
     (c)   How far up the scaffolding is the bricklayer?

4.   Claire drops a stone down a dry well. Matthew times how long it takes until it hits the bottom. Explain how this measurement of time is enough to calculate the depth of the well.

5.   A stone dropped down a well takes 1·8 s until it hits the bottom.
     How deep is the well?

6. A ball is kicked off a cliff with a horizontal velocity of 5 m/s. Two seconds later it hits the ground.

    (a) What is the vertical component of the velocity when the ball hits the ground?

    (b) Find the size of X in the diagram.

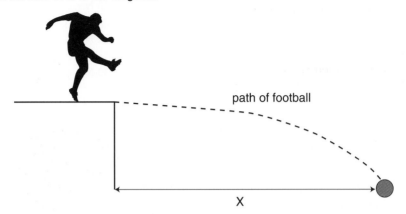

path of football

X

7. A ball is kicked off a cliff and 6 s later it hits the ground.

How far did the ball land from the base of the cliff (X) if it was kicked with a horizontal velocity of:

    (a) 2 m/s;

    (b) 4 m/s;

    (c) 7 m/s;

    (d) 8·5 m/s;

    (e) 110 cm/s?

8. An army helicopter is hovering in midair when it fires its machine guns horizontally to strike a target on the ground.

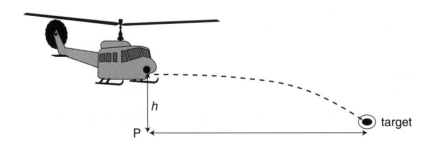

h

P

target

The horizontal velocity of the bullets is 200 m/s. If each bullet takes 4 s to reach the target;

    (a) how far is the target from point P (see diagram)?

    (b) how high is the helicopter at the time of firing (*h*)?

9. A line is fired horizontally from the top of a lighthouse to reach a ship in distress. If the ship is 100 m from the base of the lighthouse (horizontally) and the line took 3 s to reach the ship,

    (a) what is the horizontal velocity of the line when it is fired?

    (b) how high is the lighthouse?

10. In his thought experiment, Newton pictured himself at the top of a very high mountain. If he fired a projectile horizontally it would fall towards the Earth.

    (a) Under what (ideal) circumstances would the projectile go right round the Earth back to where it started?

    (b) What does this have in common with a satellite?

RE-ENTRY

1. When a space ship re-enters the Earth's atmosphere, it slows down.

    (a) This is due to friction. True or false?

    (b) Does the space ship become hot?

2. Why is the space shuttle covered in tiles?

3. When the space shuttle re-enters the Earth's atmosphere, what happens to its kinetic energy?

4. In a low orbit, the returning shuttle has a mass of approximately 75 000 kg. After it has landed, suggest a figure for its mass.

5. Silica is the preferred material to cover the shuttle.

    (a) Should its melting point be high or low?

    (b) Should its thermal conductivity be high or low?

ANSWERS

UNIT 1 — TELECOMMUNICATIONS

SECTION 1

Speed of Sound

1. Light travels faster than sound.
2. (a) Hammer makes sharp noise.
   Mic 1 detects it first and starts computer timing.
   Mic 2 detects it second and stops computer timing.
   (b) Distance between Mic 1 and Mic 2.
   Time on the computer (time for sound to travel from Mic 1 to Mic 2).
3. (a) When she sees the puff of smoke.
   (b) When she hears the bang.
   (c) Distance between herself and castle.
4. 340 m/s
5. (a) 680 m (b) 2380 m
6. (a) 5 s (b) 3 s
7. (a) 30 km (b) 90 km
8. (a) 10 s (b) 0·2 s
9. 1360 m
10. C hears A and B at the same time.
11. 510 m
12. 150 m

Waves

1.

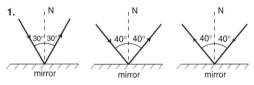

2. (a) Wave Y (b) Wave Y
3. (a) 4 m (b) 1·5 m
4. (a) 10 Hz (b) 600 waves
5. 5 cm/s or 0·05 m/s.
6. (a) 5 crests b) 7·5 cm
   (c) 45 cm/s or 0·45 m/s.

The Wave Equation

1. 2 Hz
2. 40 cm/s or 0·40 m/s.
3. 35 cm/s or 0·35 m/s.
4. 4·25 m
5. 3 cm or 0·03 m.
6. 12 Hz
7. 20 Hz
8. (a) 3 m/s (b) 0·06 m
   (c) 8·5 m. (d) 1×10^6 Hz
   (e) 0·03 m (f) 2000 Hz
9. 50 m

10. (a) 0·04 m/s (b) 1·33 Hz
11. (a) 0·02 m/s (b) 0·4 Hz
12. 1·36 m
13. 2 m
14. Velocity of A = 3 m/s.
    Velocity of B = 2·5 m/s.
    Therefore A travels faster by 0·5 m/s.
15. 50 Hz

SECTION 2

Communication Through Cables

1. (a)

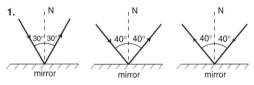

   (b) Short tap — short sound (dot).
   Long tap — long sound (dash).
   Each letter is a series of dots and dashes.
2. Yes.
3. (a) X (b) Receiver
   (c) Y (d) Transmitter
4. (a) Microphone
   (b) Sound → electrical
   (c) Loudspeaker
   (d) Electrical → sound
5. D almost 3×10^8 m/s.
6. (a) Same frequency.
   (b) Sound Q is louder than sound P.
7. (a) Both sounds have same loudness (volume).
   (b) Sound S has a higher frequency than sound R. (Actually double the frequency.)
8. True.

Reflection

1.

2.

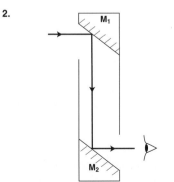

3. *(a)*

(b)

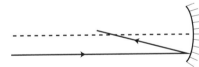

(c)

4.

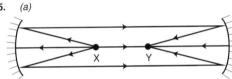

5. *(a)*

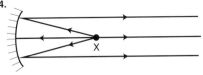

(b) Yes.
(c) Bursts into flames.
(d) Yes.

Refraction

1. *(a)*

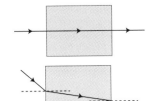

(b)

2. *(a)*

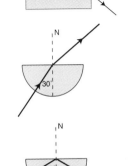

(b)

3. *(a)* The angle beyond which the light will not escape from the glass.
(b) Diagram *(b)*.

4.

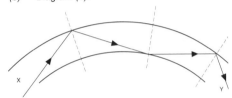

5. Optical fibres guide light to all parts of the tree. (Light is totally internally reflected along the optical fibre until it reaches the end — which is bright.)
6. Sound → electrical → light (in optical fibre). Light → electrical → sound.
7. 5×10^{-5} s
8. Standard copper wire.

SECTION 3

Radio and Television

1. *(a)* Aerial — Tuner — Decoder — ☐ —

— Loudspeaker

(b) Makes it stronger.
(c) The battery.
2. *(a)* Converts radio waves into electrical waves.
(b) To select one radio station.
(c) Electrical → sound.
3. Metal downpipe behaves like a large aerial. Bigger aerial means stronger signal — larger current — amplified — louder sound.
4. *(a)* Perfect reception.
(b) Reception becomes poor — output "crackles".
(c) Croc-clip + file produce a second wave which is causing interference with the radio wave.
5. *(a)* Signal is not reaching the car aerial because bridge is blocking it.
(b) Tape player generates a signal from inside the car.
6. *(a)* Oscilloscope 1.
(b)

7. . . . lorry because it carries the audio wave (the D.J.'s voice) from London to Glasgow.
8. *(a)* X *(b)* Y
(c) Z *(d)* X + Y = Z

9.

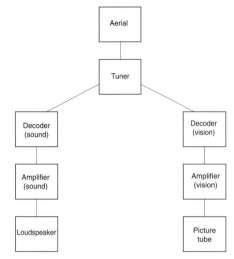

10. *(a)* To select one channel.
    (b) Electrical → light or KE → light.

11.

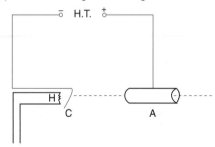

12. *(a)* A white spot in the centre.
    (b) KE → light.
13. *(a)* Yes.
    (b) Anode is hollow / electrons are travelling too fast to stop.
    (c) Increase voltage / electrons travel faster / more electrons per second strike the screen / brighter.
14. 625
15. 25
16. 0·04 seconds.
17. The human eye retains the image of one picture on the retina for a fraction of a second.
18. *(a)* A sequence of drawings which are almost identical are passed quickly one on top of the other (flick book).
       The human eye retains the image of the first picture until the second picture is in place.
    (b) A sequence of pictures which are almost identical are passed quickly onto the TV screen.
       The human eye retains the image of the first picture until the second picture is in place.
19. 1
20. 3
21. Red, green, blue.
22. Yellow. Magenta. Cyan. White.

SECTION 4

Transmission of Radio Waves

1. $D = 3 \times 10^8$ m/s
2. *(a)* $t = 2 \times 10^{-3}$ s
    (b) $t = 3 \times 10^{-3}$ s
3. $1·33 \times 10^{-4}$ s
4. *(a)* $1·15 \times 10^6$ Hz or 1·15 MHz
    (b) 2·93 m
    (c) Frequency modulated.
5. 6×10^{-2} m or 0·06 m

Diffraction

1. *(a)*   *(b)*

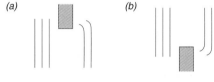

   (c)   *(d)*

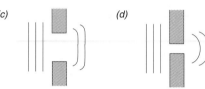

2. *(a)*   *(b)*

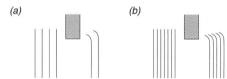

   (c) *(a)* Greater.
3. *(a)* Yes.   *(b)* Yes.
    (c) Radio waves diffract round the hills to reach the aerial on the house.
    (d) Having shorter wavelengths, TV waves diffract less than radio waves. Therefore they do not reach the aerial on the house.
4. *(a)* Yes.
    (b) Signals come from a satellite in space so the hills do not get in the way.
    (c) Yes.
    (d) Radio waves are still diffracting enough round the hills to reach the aerial on the house.
5. *(a)* The long wavelength radio waves diffract round the earth to reach America.
    (b) Long.

Satellites

1. (a) Greater   (b) Short
   (c) Long
2. (a) A satellite which remains at the same point above the earth as it orbits.
   (b) 24 hours   (c) True
3. (a) At the ground station, the signal comes from the focal point and reflects off the dish aerial. A parallel beam is sent towards the satellite.
   (b) At the satellite, one dish aerial reflects the incoming beam to a focal point where a detector is ready to receive it.

4. (a) Signal transmitted from Britain to satellite receiving dish.
   Signal collected then amplified.
   Signal transmitted from satellite to America.
   Signal collected at ground station in America.
   (b) We could bounce it off 1 reflector. If we did, it would be too weak to be detected.
   (c) An amplifier.
5. (a) To make the signal stronger. Otherwise it would be too weak to reach America.
   (b) The two frequencies are different in order to avoid interference.

UNIT 2 — ELECTRICITY

SECTION 1

From the Wall Socket

1.

Bulb	Electrical → light
Cooker	Electrical → heat
Hairdryer	Electrical → heat + kinetic
Electric fire	
Electric drill	Electrical → kinetic
Vacuum cleaner	Electrical → kinetic
Kettle	Electrical → heat

2.

Electric fire	2 kW
Bulb (bedside)	40 W
Electric drill	1500 W
TV	500 W
Hairdryer	1200 W
Kettle	2·5 kW
Cooker	12 kW

3. The current to a cooker (when everything is on) is greater than 13 A. Therefore it needs a heavy cable and a large fuse.
4. (a) A   (b) D   (c) D   (d) B
5. (a) 13 A   (b) 3 A   (c) 3 A   (d) 13 A
6. (a) Earth   (b) Neutral   (c) Live
7. (a) Green and yellow
   (b) Blue   (c) Brown.
8. (a) Yes.
   (b) If a fault occurred and the fuse blew, the appliance would still be connected to a high voltage.
9. To keep electrical contact away from water.
10..

11. Earth wire.

12. (a) Electricity flows to earth.
   (b) Fuse blows.
   (c) Casing of fire remains live. Fuse does not blow.
13. Vacuum cleaner has an electric motor. Initial current is high.

SECTION 2

A.C. and D.C.

1. . . . flows one way and then the opposite way.
2. DIRECT
   ALTERNATING
3. (a) 230 V   (b) 325 V
4. (a) 50 Hz   (b) 100
5.

ANSWERS

Oscilloscopes and Voltage

1. *(a)*   *(b)*

2.	*(a)* d.c.	*(b)*	15 V
3.	*(a)* a.c.	*(b)*	20 V
4.	*(a)* d.c.	*(b)*	7·5 V
5.	*(a)* a.c.	*(b)*	6·75 V

Oscilloscopes and Frequency

1. *(a)*   *(b)*

12 waves   3 waves

2.	*(a)* 50 m s = 0·05 s	*(b)*	20 Hz
3.	*(a)* 4 m s = 0·004 s	*(b)*	250 Hz
4.	*(a)* 20 m s = 0·02 s	*(b)*	50 Hz
5.	*(a)* 0·67 s	*(b)*	1·5 Hz

Charge — Current — Time

1. 60 C
2. 150 C
3. *(a)*   3 A   *(b)*   3 A
4. 2 A
5. 13 s
6. 400 s
7. 7
8. It would require 11·5 electrons. Clearly you cannot sub-divide $1·6 \times 10^{-19}$ C.

SECTIONS 3 / 4

Resistors in series

1.	30 Ω	**2.**	48 Ω	**3.**	124 Ω
4.	1180 Ω	**5.**	3 kΩ	**6.**	2·6 kΩ
7.	1·6 MΩ	**8.**	0·8 MΩ	**9.**	704 700 Ω
10.	270 Ω				

Resistors in parallel

1.	4 Ω	**2.**	20 Ω	**3.**	11·25 Ω
4.	250 Ω	**5.**	6 Ω	**6.**	10 Ω
7.	500 Ω	**8.**	5 Ω	**9.**	12 Ω
10.	2·25 Ω				

Combinations of series and parallel

1.	453 Ω	**2.**	1125 Ω	**3.**	15·33 Ω
4.	142·23 Ω	**5.**	19 Ω			

Ohm's Law (basic problems)

1.	12 V	**2.**	1·5 V	**3.**	100 V
4.	230 V	**5.**	1·33 A	**6.**	0·3 A
7.	0·115 A	**8.**	0·02 A	**9.**	4 Ω
10.	80 Ω	**11.**	40 Ω	**12.**	2300 Ω

Ohm's Law (intermediate problems)

1.	0·5 A	**2.**	2·25 A
3.	1·33 A	**4.**	75 V
5.	18 V	**6.**	230 V
7.	0·8 A, 12 V	**8.**	0·6 A, 18 V
9.	0·12 A $V_1 = 4·8$ V	**10.**	2 A, 8 V
	$V_2 = 7·2$ V		
	$V_3 = 12$ V		
	$V_4 = 24$ V		
11.	0·8 A, 48 V	**12.**	0·03 A, 5·4 V

Voltage Division

1.	$V_1 = 6$ V	**2.**	$V_1 = 8$ V
	$V_2 = 6$ V		$V_2 = 16$ V
3.	$V_1 = 14$ V	**4.**	12 V
	$V_2 = 6$ V		
	$V_3 = 4$ V		
5.	4 V	**6.**	8 V

Current Division

1.	$A_1 = 3$ A	**2.**	$A_1 = 2$ A
	$A_2 = 3$ A		$A_2 = 2$ A
			$A_3 = 4$ A
3.	$A_1 = 2$ A	**4.**	$A_1 = 1·25$ A
	$A_2 = 1$ A		$A_2 = 1·25$ A
	$A_3 = 3$ A		$A_3 = 1·25$ A
			$A_4 = 3·75$ A
			$A_5 = 2·5$ A
5.	$A_1 = 3$ A	**6.**	$A_1 = 2$ A
			$A_2 = 5$ A
			$A_3 = 3$ A
			$A_4 = 2$ A

Power and Electrical Energy

1.	*(a)*	36 W	*(b)*	575 W
	(c)	1840 W	*(d)*	92 W
2.	*(a)*	4 A	*(b)*	10 A
	(c)	0·43 A	*(d)*	4 A
3.	*(a)*	20 V	*(b)*	12 V
	(c)	230 V	*(d)*	20 V
4.	*(a)*	920 W	*(b)*	57·5 Ω
5.	*(a)*	4 A	*(b)*	3 Ω
6.	*(a)*	125 V	*(b)*	31·25 Ω

7.

	A	B	C
(a)	0·18 W	0·31 W	0·72 W
(b)	200 Ω	5 Ω	200 Ω

8. 884·62 Ω or 881·67 Ω depending on system.
9. 353·85 Ω or 352·67 Ω depending on system.

10	*(a)*	1·5 W	*(b)*	15 J
11.	*(a)*	0·6 W	*(b)*	36 J
12.	*(a)*	0·5 A	*(b)*	5 W

13. (a) 200 Ω   (b) 0·2 A
    (c) 10 V   (d) 2 W
    (e) 30 V   (f) 6 W
14. (a) 1500 Ω → 7·5 V
        2500 Ω → 12·5 V
    (b) 1500 Ω → 3.75×10^{-2} W
        2500 Ω → 6.25×10^{-2} W
15. (a) (i) 3 W   (ii) 400 W   (iii) 6 W
    (b) (i) 900 J   (ii) 120 000 J   (iii) 1800 J
16. 1380 kJ
17. (a) 3.6×10^6 J   (b) 3.6×10^6 J
18. (a) $I_1 = 0.26$ A
        $I_2 = 0.44$ A
        $I_3 = 0.87$ A
        $I_4 = 0.87$ A
    (b) 2·44 A   (c) 560 W
19. (a) 3 A   (b) 13 A
    (c) 13 A   (d) 13 A
    (e) 13 A   (f) 3 A
20. (a) 4·35 A   (b) 8·70 A
    (c) 13 A
21. 12 V
22. (a) 8 V   (b) 26·67 Ω
23. 9 Ω
24. 2 Ω

SECTION 5

Behind the Wall

1. (a) Nothing; continue to operate normally.
   (b) Nothing; continue to operate normally.
2. (a) A_1.
   (b) In the ring circuit, the current has two paths to travel.
3. The current in each wire is smaller.
   Connecting cable can be thinner (smaller power rating cable).
4. (a) Three.
   (b) Perfectly adequate to cover the current drawn from the sockets.
       Highly unlikely that all sockets would be in use at the same time — even then they would all have to be delivering high currents simultaneously!
   (c) Current to the cooker exceeds 13 A when all parts of the cooker are on.
       Individual plug fuse is 13 A (max).
   (d) Ring mains wire is thicker than wire used for the lighting circuit.
5. (a) Current was too high. Automatic cut out.
   (b) Current now low (below the threshold to "pop" the button).
   (c) It can be reset easily. When a fuse wire melts — we need a new fuse.

The Kilowatt-hour

6. (a) 10 kW h   (b) 80 p
7 (a) 20 kW h   (b) £1.60
8. (a) 1·6 kW h   (b) 12·8 pence
9. (a) 0·2 kW h   (b) 1·6 pence
10.   100 W bulb costs 3·6 pence.
       1200 W heater costs 4·8 pence.
       ∴ heater costs more to run (1·2 pence more).

SECTION 6

Movement from Electricity

1. (a) NORTH   to   SOUTH
   (b) P   or   R   at   Q
   (c) P   and   R
2. (a)

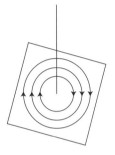

   (b) Compass needle would move to point to magnetic north.
3. 1. Increase current (bigger supply).
   2. Increase number of turns.
   3. Insert a soft iron core into the coil.
4. (a) Gap closes.   (b) A magnetic field.
   (c) (E.g.) Control circuit for a high-power electric motor.
5. (a) Magnetic field round the copper wire interacts with permanent field to produce a force which pushes the wire along the two runners.
   (b) Opposite from part (a).
6. (a) Force reversed (now downwards).
   (b) Downwards (opposite of diagram).
7. (a) Downwards.
   (b) Zero (wire does not cut any lines of force).
8. (a) P R A B C D S Q
   (b) P S D C B A R Q
9. (a) Reverses the current every half cycle in order to maintain rotation in one direction.
   (b) Good conductor of electricity.
       Soft.
10. (a) They can provide a stronger magnetic field.
    (b) The more coils there are, the smoother the rotation of the electric motor.

UNIT 3 — HEALTH PHYSICS

SECTION 1

The Use of Thermometers

1. (a) — 10 °C → 110 °C
    (b)   35 °C → 43 °C
    (c) Laboratory thermometer.
    (d) Measuring human body temperature.
2. (a) Reading drops immediately.
    (b) Reading stays at 40 °C and then slowly drops.
    (c) To slow down the rate of flow of the mercury.
3. (a) It is pressed onto the baby's forehead.
    (b) The baby could break the glass of a clinical thermometer.
4. (a) Expand
         Move   Gap
         Complete
    (b) X
5. Rototherm
6. Rototherm   →   angle of deflection
    Mercury   →   length of liquid column
    Thermocouple →   voltage

SECTION 2

Using Sound

1. (a) Yes   (b) Yes   (c) Yes   (d) Yes
2. Molecules in a solid are closer together than they are in a gas.
3. A = open bell   B = closed bell
    C = valve   D = diaphragm
4. Open bell — low frequency — heart sounds.
    Closed bell — high frequency — lung sounds.
5. (a) 80 Hz   (b) Lungs   (c) Closed bell.
6. (a) 600 m   (b) 300 m
7. (a) Some ultrasound is lost.
    (b) 150 m   (c) 75 m
8.

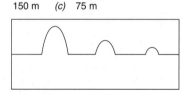

9. (a) 0·15 m   (b) 0·075 m or 7.5×10^{-2} m
10. (a) 0·012 m or 1.2×10^{-2} m
    (b) X-rays kill cells and could damage the baby.
11.

Noise level /dB
110
90
130
60

12. 140 dB
13. 20 Hz → 20 000 Hz
14. (a) 22 kHz   (b) 0·015 m or 1.5×10^{-2} m
15. (a) 255 m   (b) 25·5 s

SECTION 3

Light and Sight

1.

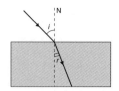

2.

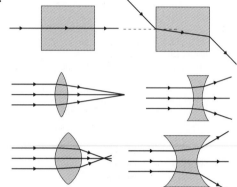

3.

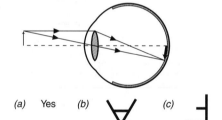

    (a) Yes   (b)   ∀   (c)   ⌐

4. (a) Long sighted   (b) Yes
5. (a) Short sighted   (b) Yes
6. (a)

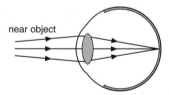

    near object

    (b) Second diagram

154

7.

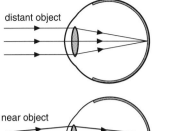

distant object

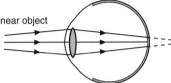

near object

8.

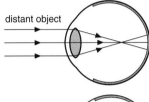

distant object

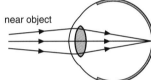

near object

9.

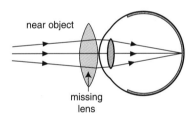

near object

missing
lens

10.

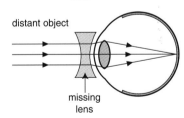

distant object

missing
lens

Power of a Lens

1. 5 D   **2.** 3·33 D
3. *(a)* 20 D   *(b)* 10 D   *(c)* Lens (a) 5 cm
4. –5 D   **5.** –4 D
6. *(a)* – 10 cm   *(b)* – 25 cm
     (c) Lens (a) – 10 D
7. *(a)* 25 cm   *(b)* Convex
8. *(a)* – 12·5 cm   *(b)* Concave

Use of Fibre Optics in Medicine

1.

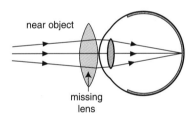

2. $1·5 \times 10^{-8}$ s
3. One bundle takes light to the patient. One bundle takes (reflected) light back to the doctor.
4. Much smaller wounds / sometimes no wound at all / less dangerous to the patient.
5. *(a)* Hot lamp is kept outside patient. Light travelling down is cold.
     (b) No chance of burning delicate tissue.

SECTION 4

Using the Spectrum

1. Carbon dioxide laser.
2. *(a)* Yes.   *(b)* Endoscope.
3. *(a)* A laser which just vapourises surface tissue.
     (b) It has a shallow penetration.
4. *(a)* Argon laser.
     (b) Heating blood vessels until they clot.
     (c) Blood vessels can grow forward and bleed into the eye due to a lack of oxygen. Photocoagulation clots these blood vessels. Retina now requires less oxygen.
5. 20 W
6. To prevent any reflections of the laser light since it can damage the human eye.
7. Photographic film.
8. Black.
9. 3-dimensional analysis.
10. *(a)* 6×10^{-8} m   *(b)* $3·33 \times 10^{-8}$ m
     (c) X-ray *(b)*.
11. U.V. is absorbed by the skin to produce vitamin D3.
12. Skin cancer.
13. *(a)* 1×10^{15} Hz   *(b)* $8·57 \times 10^{14}$ Hz
     (c) U.V. wave *(a)*.
14. *(a)* Infrared waves.
     (b) (i) Yes.   (ii) Yes.
15. *(a)* Arnie's body.   *(b)* No.
     (c) Infrared rays coming from his body cannot get through the mud.
16. Yes — the lights emit I.R.
17. *(a)* A type of photograph based on I.R. rays.
     (b) Hotter than the surrounding tissue.
18. *(a)* $7·5 \times 10^{13}$ Hz   *(b)* $6·67 \times 10^{13}$ Hz
     (c) Infrared wave *(a)*.

SECTION 5

Nuclear Radiation — Humans and Medicine

1. *(a)* 11   *(b)* 11   *(c)* 12   *(d)* Nucleus.
2. *(a)* 11 protons cancel out 11 electrons.
     (b) +1
3. *(a)* Stripping electrons off uncharged atoms creates charged particles (ions).
     (b) **Alpha particle** is slow, heavy — makes many collisions with (air) molecules — a lot of ionisation.
     Beta particle is fast and light — makes few collisions with (air) molecules — not a lot of ionisation.

ANSWERS

4.

Type	Description	Mass	Charge
α	Helium nucleus 2p + 2n	4 a.m.u.	+2
β	Fast electron	$\frac{1}{1836}$ a.m.u.	−1
γ	High frequency, high energy wave	0	0

5. . . . beta . . .   . . . alpha . . .
. . . beta particles have long range but low ionising power.
. . . alpha particles have short range but high ionising power.

6. *(a)* Gamma.
(b) Does not cause enough ionisation.

7. *(a)* To allow alpha particles to enter.
(b) Low.   *(c)* Argon.
(d) Radiation enters window / causes ionisation / electrons strike uncharged gas molecules creating further ionisation / more electrons produced — avalanche / one spark inside tube / one current in circuit / one count on scalar.

8. There is radiation all round us.
The teacher detected the **background** count.

9.

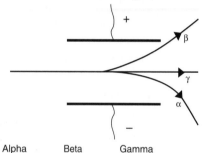

10. Alpha   Beta   Gamma

Half Life

1. The time taken for a radioactive material to decay to half its original value.

2. *(a)* 80 c.p.m.   *(b)* 40 c.p.m.
(c) 20 c.p.m.   *(d)* 20 days.

3. *(a)* 64 c.p.m.   *(b)* 32 c.p.m.
(c) 16 c.p.m.   *(d)* 30 days.

4. *(a)* (i) 40 c.p.m.   (ii) 20 c.p.m.
(iii) 10 c.p.m.   (iv) 5 c.p.m.

(b)

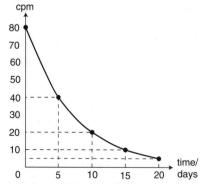

(c) (i) Approx. 15 c.p.m.   (ii) Approx. 7 c.p.m.

5. *(a)* (i) 100 c.p.m.   (ii) 50 c.p.m.
(iii) 25 c.p.m.   (iv) 12·5 c.p.m.

(b)

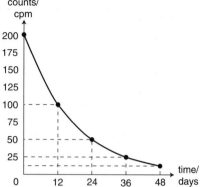

(c) (i) Approx. 77 c.p.m.   (ii) Approx. 20 c.p.m.

6. *(a)* (i) 120 c.p.m.   (ii) 60 c.p.m.
(iii) 30 c.p.m.   (iv) 15 c.p.m.

(b)

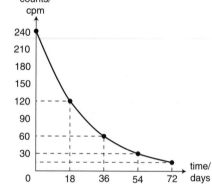

(c) (i) Approx. 50 c.p.m. (ii) Approx. 170 c.p.m.

7. Approx. 3·25 days.

8. 144 c.p.m.

9. 20 minutes.

10. *(a)* 5600 years.   *(b)* 11 200 years.

UNIT 4 — ELECTRONICS

SECTION 1

Overview

1. *(a)*
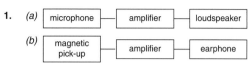

(b)

2. Output is **continuously** variable.
3. Output is **not continuous**, i.e., it is in steps, e.g. 1, 2, 3, 4, etc.
4. Digital.
5.

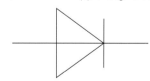

SECTION 2

Output Devices

1. *(a)* Electrical → sound.
   (b) Electrical → kinetic.
   (c) Electrical → kinetic.
   (d) Electrical → kinetic.
   (e) Electrical → light.

2.

Analogue	Digital
Loudspeaker	Solenoid
Electric motor	Relay
	L.E.D

3. *(a)* Loudspeaker. *(b)* L.E.D.
   (c) Solenoid. *(d)* 7-segment display.
4. *(a)*

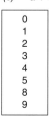

   (b) Above symbol should be added in the gap (this way round).
5. To protect it from large currents (resistor cuts down the current).
6. *(a)* 3 V *(b)* 30 Ω
7. *(a)* 4 V *(b)* 80 Ω
8. 190 Ω
9. *(a)* a f e d c g *(b)* a f g c d
   (c) a f e d c b
10.

0
1
2
3
4
5
8
9

SECTION 3

Input Devices

Thermistors and LDRs

1. *(a)* Sound → electrical.
   (b) Heat → electrical.
   (c) Light → electrical.
2. 150 Ω   3. 200 Ω
4. *(a)* 0·05 A   *(b)* 0·2 A
5. *(a)* 0·01 A   *(b)* 0·16 A
6. $6 \cdot 25 \times 10^{-4}$ A   7. $3 \cdot 85 \times 10^{-4}$ A
8. 3·75 V   9. 1·25 V
10. *(a)* 0·45 V   *(b)* 4·17 V

Capacitor Circuits

1. Energy
2. *(a)* 5 V   *(b)* 0 A
3. *(a)* 5 V   *(b)* 0 V
4. *(a)* Greater than 10 s. *(b)* Less than 10 s.
5. *(a)* Less than 9 s. *(b)* Greater than 9 s.
6. Circuit same as question 5 with voltmeter replaced with camera input.
7. *(a)*
   (b)

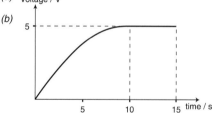

   c) As each electron goes on to the capacitor plate it gets harder and harder due to the repulsion of existing electrons, i.e., it takes longer to put the last electron on compared to the first electron.

Voltage Dividers — A

1. 1 V   2. 4 V   3. 2 V   4. 1·67 V
5. 4·55 V   6. 0 → 1·25 V

Voltage Dividers — B

1.	Decreases	2.	Decreases
	Decreases		Decreases
			Increases
			Increases
3.	Decreases	4.	Decreases
	Decreases		Decreases
	Decreases		Increases
			Increases

ANSWERS

SECTION 4

Digital Processes

The Transistor as a switch

1. Decreases
   Off

2. Decreases
   Increases
   Increases
   On

3. Decreases
   Decreases
   Increases
   Increases
   On

4. Increases
   Increases
   Increases
   On

Logic Gates

1.

A	B	Output
0	0	0
0	1	0
1	0	0
1	1	1

2.

A	B	Output
0	0	0
0	1	1
1	0	1
1	1	1

3.

Input	Output
0	1
1	0

4.

A	B	X	Output
0	0	0	1
0	1	0	1
1	0	0	1
1	1	1	0

5.

A	B	Output
0	0	0
0	1	0
1	0	1
1	1	0

6.

A	B	Output
0	0	1
0	1	0
1	0	1
1	1	1

7.

A	B	C	Output
0	0	0	0
0	0	1	0
0	1	0	0
1	0	0	0
0	1	1	1
1	0	1	1
1	1	0	0
1	1	1	1

8.

A	B	C	Output
0	0	0	0
0	0	1	0
0	1	0	0
1	0	0	0
0	1	1	0
1	0	1	0
1	1	0	1
1	1	1	0

9. (a) Switch is on. Light detector low (darkness).
   (b) Lamp comes on automatically when it becomes dark.

10.

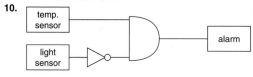

The Clock Pulse Generator

1. (a) 5 V (b) 5 V, 0, 0 (c) Yes
2. Initially capacitor uncharged.
   X is logic 0; Y is logic 1; Z is logic 1.
   ∴ capacitor charges up through resistor until full.
   ∴ X is now logic 1; Y is now logic 0; Z is now logic 0.
   ∴ Capacitor discharges.
   This cycle repeats itself.
3. (a) Longer time. (b) Frequency is reduced.
4. (a) Longer time. (b) Frequency is reduced.
5. Digital.

SECTION 5

Analogue Processes

1. (a) To increase the amplitude of the signal.
   (b) The battery.
2.

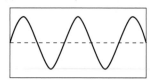

3. (a) Yes.
   (b) No — amplitude larger after amplification.

Voltage Gain

4. 15 5. 20 6. 50 7. 8 V
8. 0·4 V 9. 14·4 W 10. 2 W 11. 40 V

Power Gain

12. 9 13. 50 14. 50
15. 50 W 16. 0·25 W

UNIT 5 — TRANSPORT

SECTION 1

Distance, Speed and Time

Average Speed

1 24 m
2. 22·5 m
3. 80 s = 1 min 20 s
4. 201 s = 3 min 21 s
5. 80 m/s
6. 106·67 km/h
7. 10 m/s
8. *(a)* 720 m   *(b)* 2052 m
9. *(a)* 420 m   *(b)* 60 m
10. *(a)* 10 km   *(b)* 5 km/h
11. 36 km/h   **12.** 32·5 km/h
13. 6·82 m/s   **14.** 8 min 16 s
15. 510 m

Instantaneous Speed

1. 0·30 m/s
2. *(a)* 0·08 m/s   *(b)* 0·8 m/s
       (c) 1 m/s   *(d)* 4 m/s
3. *(a)* Need to add light gate and timer (train cuts light beam).
       (b) Length of train.
              Time on timer.
       (c) $v = \dfrac{\text{length of train}}{\text{time on the timer}}$
4. *(a)* 0·8 m/s
       (b) Anything less than 0·25 s.
       (c) No — not accurate enough due to human reaction time.
5. No — cannot guarantee a diameter of the ball will go through the light beam.

Acceleration 1

1. *(a)* 8 m/s   *(b)* 12 m/s
       (c) 20 m/s   *(d)* 22 m/s
2. *(a)* 10 m/s   *(b)* 20 m/s
       (c) 30 m/s   *(d)* 35 m/s
3. 5 m/s^2 **4.** 2 m/s^2
5. 0·5 m/s^2 **6.** 2·25 m/s^2
7. 3·55 m/s^2 **8.** 4·66 m/s^2
9. Acceleration = −160 m/s^2
       ∴ Deceleration = 160 m/s^2
10. *(a)* 0·5 m/s^2 *(b)* 6 s
11. *(a)* 0·4 cm/s^2 *(b)* 2·0 cm/s
12. *(a)* 0·25 m/s^2 *(b)* 6·25 m/s
       (c) 26 s
13. *(a)* 4 cm/s   *(b)* 12 cm
       (c) 2·67 cm/s^2
14. *(a)* 3 m/s^2 *(b)* 6 m/s
       (c) 24 m
15. 5 cm/s
16. Car is 10 m ahead of athlete.

Acceleration 2

Light Gates

1. *(a)* 0·5 m/s   *(b)* 0·17 m/s^2
2. *(a)* 0·25 m/s   *(b)* 0·50 m/s
       (c) 0·10 m/s^2

3. *(a)* 0·40 m/s   *(b)* 1·00 m/s
       (c) 0·33 m/s^2
4. *(a)* 0·50 m/s   *(b)* 0·75 m/s
       (c) 2·08 m/s^2
       (d) No — human reaction time is too large to time such a short time accurately.

Speed / Time Graphs

1. 4 m/s^2
2. *(a)*

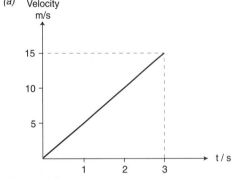

       (b) 5 m/s^2
3. *(a)*

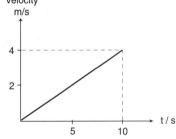

       (b) 0·4 m/s^2
4. *(a)*

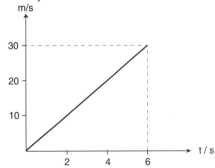

       (b) 5 m/s^2
5. *(a)* 2 m/s   *(b)* 4 m/s^2
       (c) 7·5 m/s^2 *(d)* C
       (e) Bigger
              Bigger
6. *(a)* 40 m   *(b)* 10 m/s

7. (a) 54 m (b) 9 m/s
8. (a) 78 m (b) 13 m/s
9. (a) 105 m (b) 10·5 m/s
10. (a) 110 m (b) 10 m/s
(c) 2·5 m/s^2, 2·5 m/s^2
11. (a) 5 m/s^2 (b) −10 m/s^2
(c) 140 m (d) 14 m/s
12. (a) 3 m/s^2 (b) −6 m/s^2
(c) 108 m (d) 9 m/s
13. (a) 2·5 m/s^2 (b) 5 m/s^2
(c) 135 m (d) 13·5 m/s
14. (a) 0·13 m/s^2 (b) 0·27 m/s^2
(c) 150 m (d) 3·33 m/s
15. (a) 270 m
(b) Does not include driver's reaction time / reaction distance.

SECTION 2

Forces and Friction

1. 700 N
2. (a) 10 N (b) 50 N
(c) 520 N (d) 12 000 N
(e) 1 N
3. (a) 40 N (b) 110 N
(c) 180 N (d) 212 N
4. (a) 1·67 N/kg
(b) Six times faster on earth.
5. (a) 800 N (b) 304 N
(c) Far away from planets.
Still has a mass of 80 kg.
6. E.g. 1. Air table — air lifts disc.
2. Polystyrene beads — a book slides easily over the beads.
7. (a) Spread himself out ⇒ max surface area.
(b) Make himself streamlined ⇒ min surface area.
8. (a) Put head in water / less splashing.
(b) Smooth — cut down friction.
9. (a) Audi 100 (b) Austin Mini
10. When force forward equals force backward (friction caused by tyres and air resistance).

Newton's First Law

1. A body stays at rest or moves at constant velocity (in a straight line) unless an unbalanced force acts on it.
2. (a) Yes.
(b) The hammer has mass.
The moving mass strikes helmet creating a force on the helmet.
3. (a) Lifts the disc — cuts down friction.
(b) Disc would travel slowly due to the increase in friction.
4. The bus stops but the people are not strapped in.
The people continue to move at constant velocity.
5. (a) Parachute catches a lot of air — increases friction.

(b)

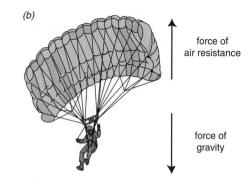

force of air resistance

force of gravity

Newton's Second Law

1. 12 N   2. 3600 N
3. 12 m/s^2 4. 6 m/s^2
5. 4 kg
6. (a) 16 kg
(b) Object falling on Earth.
7.

Answer
909 N
15 000 kg
6·4 m/s^2
400 kg
7000 N

8. 8 m/s^2
9. (a) 8 m/s^2 (b) 24 m/s
10. (a) 7 N (b) 3·5 m/s^2
(c) To the right. (d) 10·5 m/s
11. (a) 6 N to the right. (b) 4 m/s^2
(c) 14 m/s
12. (a) 4 m/s^2 (b) 3·6 N
13. (a) 5 m/s^2 (b) 15 kg
14. (a) 3720 N
(b) Force forward must overcome friction.
Force forward = unbalanced force + friction force
15. (a) 4 m/s^2 (b) 6000 N
16. (a) 5 m/s^2 (b) 9000 N
(c) −7·5 m/s^2
(d) 13 500 N against the car.
17. (a) 0·5 m/s^2 (b) 125 N
(c) 0 N
18. 800 N
19. (a) 90 N (b) 180 N (up)
(c) 20 m/s^2 (up)
20. 10 m/s^2 (up)

SECTION 3

Work Done and Power

1.	10 000 J	**2.**	1200 J
3.	20 N	**4.**	110 N
5.	5 m	**6.**	500 m
7.	*(a)* 60 J *(b)* 12 W	**8.**	125 W
9.	1920 W	**10.**	168 W
11.	*(a)* 10 J *(b)* 10 J	**12.**	672 W
13.	*(a)* 3240 J	*(b)*	1080 J
14.	*(a)* 60 000 J	*(b)*	12 000 J
15.	*(a)* 4000 J	*(b)*	16 000 J
	(c) Some energy is converted into heat (and sound) due to friction.		

Potential and Kinetic Energy

1.	2500 J	**2.**	600 J
3.	34 m	**4.**	0·5 m
5.	2·5 kg	**6.**	4 kg
7.	*(a)* 400 J *(b)* 600 J *(c)* 200 J *(d)* 750 J Mass is 5 kg.		
8.	875 J	**9.**	720 J
10.	0·5 kg	**11.**	1000 kg
12.	25 m/s	**13.**	10 m/s

14. 1334·7 J

15. *(a)* B *(b)* A and C
(c) Converted into heat (due to friction).

16. *(a)* 1 J *(b)* 1 J *(c)* 2 m/s

17. 1·41 m/s **18.** 4·8 J

19. 20 m/s **20.** 20 m/s

21. The impact velocity of two different masses dropped from the same height is the same, i.e. impact velocity is independent of mass.

22. *(a)* 45 m *(b)* 30 m/s (downwards)

23. *(a)* 15 m/s^2 *(b)* 45 m/s
(c) 4050 J

24. *(a)* 4 m/s^2 *(b)* 20 m/s ; 6000 J
(c) 20 m

25. *(a)* The ball had K.E. when it left John's hand which adds to the P.E. Therefore when it bounces higher it comes to a (momentary) stop, i.e. **all** the energy is potential energy.

(b) The horizontal velocity of the shell does not change but the vertical velocity does.
At point X the vertical velocity is zero, i.e. as the P.E. of the shell increases, the vertical velocity decreases.
The horizontal velocity remains constant throughout.

UNIT 6 — ENERGY MATTERS

SECTION 1

Supply and Demand

1. Coal, oil, nuclear.

2. For example, cavity wall insulation, double glazing, etc.

3. Saves petrol (one car replacing two).

4. The foreman is right. The electricity bill will not change because the fluorescent tube burns the same electricity as the bulb.

5.

Renewable	Non-renewable
solar	coal
wind	oil
hydroelectric	nuclear
	gas

6. *(a)* Light → electrical *(b)* More
(c) Tilting the arms so that the surface is at 90˚ to the Sun's rays gives MAX surface area and MAX electricity produced.

7. *(a)* Temperature increases.
(b) To increase the surface area of pipe (water) exposed to the lamp's rays.

8. The "fins" provide a large surface area for the air to cool the engine.

9. *(a)* Cannot generate electricity at night.
(b) Erratic production of electricity due to varying wind.
(c) Very few suitable available sites.

10. *(a)* Cheap *(b)* Clean *(c)* Renewable (any order)

11. *(a)* 3 kw h *(b)* 72 kw h

12. *(a)* 800 W *(b)* 4000 W
(c) Not all the energy is transferred into the house.

SECTION 2

Generation of Electricity

1. *(a)* Chemical → heat
(b) Kinetic → electrical

2. *(a)* Potential energy
(b) Potential → kinetic
(c) Kinetic → electrical

3. *(a)* Oil, coal.
(b) Oil, coal, nuclear.

4. *(a)* Water gains speed as it flows down the mountain (potential → kinetic). The fast flowing water hits fins on the water turbine causing it to spin. The water turbine turns a generator which produces electricity.
(b) Low demand for electricity at night. Water is still flowing down the mountain so it is producing electricity which is not required.
(c) Water is pumped up to a reservoir so that it is available to produce electricity at times of peak demand

5. (a) 2.8×10^7 J (b) $\dfrac{3.21 \times 10^6}{1}$

6.

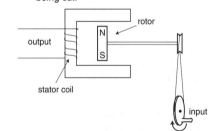

7. (a) 3240 J (b) 1080 J (c) 33.33%
8. (a) 81 J (b) 30 J (c) 37%
9. (a) 12 000 J (b) 8000 J (c) 66.67%
10. (a) 3200 J (b) 2400 J (c) 75%
(d) 320 W

SECTION 3

Electromagnetic Induction and the Transformer

1. (a) Reading goes to zero.
(b) Reading changes from zero to –5 on the scale.
(c) Reading goes to zero.
(d) Moving the magnet quickly produces a larger current (but for a shorter time).
2. (a) Reading would be larger than +5.
(b) Reading would be larger than +5.
3. (a) Yes. (b) No.
(c) Current only produced when lines of force are being cut.
4.

output — rotor — N S — stator coil — input

5. Spinning the rotor means lines of force are cutting the stator coils. Current is produced in the coil.
6. 1. Permanent magnet rotor is replaced with an electromagnet.
2. The stator is not one coil but several coils.
7. (a) Same magnetic field links both coils.
(b) a.c.
(c) There would be no current (bulb off) in the secondary circuit (apart from a momentary current when supply is connected).
D.c. source does not produce a changing current / changing field necessary to generate electricity in the secondary coils.

8. (a) Yes.
(b) Increase number of coils.
Replace wooden rod with soft iron core.
Replace a.c. supply with a high current supply.
(c) It will increase.
9. *Observation 1.* Coil is producing a magnetic pole the same as the magnet (e.g. two north poles) — repel.
Observation 2. Coil is producing a magnetic pole the same as the magnet (e.g. two north poles) — repel.
Reversing the terminals would cause the coil to **attract** the permanent magnet in both cases.
10. Copper loss — heating of the metal coils.
Eddy currents — currents set up within the metal core.
Hysteresis loss — energy loss in magnetising and demagnetising coil.

Transformers and Voltage

1. 50 V **2.** 160 V
3. 16 V **4.** 50 T
5. 16 T **6.** 2800 T
7. 200 T **8.** 400 T
9. 600 T **10.** 120 V
11. 360 V **12.** 50 V

Transformers and Power

1. (a) 25 V (b) 2 A (c) 0.4 A
2. (a) 250 V (b) 125 V (c) 8 A
3. (a) 1000 V (b) 4 A in each bar
(c) 2 A
4. (a) 500 V (b) 250 V
(c) A current flowing in the power line has a heating effect due to the resistance in the wire. The bigger the current, the bigger the heating effect and the more energy wasted. A high power can be obtained by using a low current and a high voltage. Less energy is wasted due to a smaller heating effect.
5. (a) 12 000 turns (b) 460 W
(c) 3 A
6. (a) 1000 W (b) 1000 V (c) 1 A
(d) 8 A (e) 2 A
7. (a) 200 V (b) 5 mA
8. (a) 2 A (b) 3.5 A (c) 4.5 A
9. (a) 40 V (b) 30 V (c) 25 Ω
10. (a) 24 V (b) 16 V (c) 0.33 A
(d) 2.64 W

SECTION 4

Specific Heat Capacity

1. It takes 4180 J to raise the temperature of 1 kg of water by 1 ˚C.
2. (a) 12 540 J (b) 20 900 J
(c) 10 450 J
3. (a) 167 200 J (b) 180 400 J
(c) 57 900 J (d) 2560 J
4. (a) 1.20 ˚C (b) 4.43 ˚C
(c) 43.18 ˚C (d) 2.84 ˚C

5. *(a)* 0·24 kg   *(b)* 1·11 kg
    (c) 2·59 kg   *(d)* 0·43 kg
6. *(a)* 259·07 ˚C   *(b)* 256·48 ˚C
7. *(a)* 1003·2 s or 16 minutes 43·2 s
    (b) The actual time will be longer due to heat losses in the kettle and the surrounding air.
8. *(a)* 25 080 J   *(b)* 772 J
    (c) 8 minutes 37·04 s
9. *(a)* 355 300 J
    (b) 80% : 444 125 J
    (c) Some heats the kettle body and some is lost to the surroundings.
10. *(a)* 6 ˚C   *(b)* 2500 J
    (c) 416·67 J/kg ˚C
    (d) Not all the heat energy goes into the copper, some goes into the atmosphere, the heater element itself and even the thermometer.
11. *(a)* 110 400 J   *(b)* 24·48 ˚C
    (This assumes no heat energy is lost to the surroundings.)
12. *(a)* 7600 J   *(b)* 5790 J
    (c) 76·18%

Specific Latent Heat

1. *(a)* To break down the bonds between molecules.
    (b) The energy required to change the state of 1 kg of the substance.
    (c) *Fusion:* energy required to change 1 kg of substance from solid to liquid.
       Vaporisation: energy required to change 1 kg of substance from liquid to gas.
2. *(a)* Liquid to gas.   *(b)* Compressor pump.
3. Liquid inside the rollers is changing state back to a solid at constant temperature.
4. 868 400 J
5. 5 876 000 J
6. *(a)* $13 \cdot 36 \times 10^5$ J   *(b)* $16 \cdot 72 \times 10^5$ J
    (c) $9 \cdot 04 \times 10^6$ J   *(b)* $1 \cdot 20 \times 10^7$ J
7. $5 \cdot 7 \times 10^6$ J
8. *(a)* 0·08 kg   *(b)* 28 000 J
    (c) $3 \cdot 5 \times 10^5$ J/kg
    (d) Not all the electrical energy goes into the ice. Some energy is lost to the heater and the surroundings.
9. 27 minutes 50 seconds.
10. *(a)* 1 171 520 J   *(b)* 80% : 1 464 400 J
    (c) 12 minutes 12 seconds.

UNIT 7 — SPACE

SECTION 1 — SIGNALS FROM SPACE

The Light Year

1. *(a)* Planet   *(b)* Planet
    (c) Star.
2. 9
3. Yes
4. *(a)* 6×10^8 m   *(b)* 9×10^9 m
    (c) $1 \cdot 8 \times 10^{10}$ m
5. *(a)* $1 \cdot 08 \times 10^{12}$ m   *(b)* $2 \cdot 59 \times 10^{13}$ m
    (c) $9 \cdot 46 \times 10^{15}$ m
6. $9 \cdot 46 \times 10^{15}$ m
7. $t = \dfrac{d}{v} = \dfrac{1 \cdot 5 \times 10^{11} \text{ m}}{3 \times 10^8 \text{ m/s}}$ = 500 s
                = 8 mins 20 s
8. 760 s = 12 mins 40 s
9. *(a)* $7 \cdot 8 \times 10^7$ km   *(b)* 4 mins 20 s
10. $4 \cdot 07 \times 10^{16}$ m

Refracting Telescope

1. *(a)*

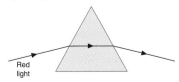

objective   eyepiece

    (b) Yes
2. *(a)* Brighter.
    (b) More light enters objective lens.

3. *(a)* and *(b)*

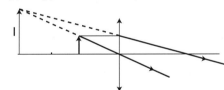

    (c) Virtual / Magnified / Erect.
4. *(a)* Diagram as question 3.
    (b) 5 cm (approx.)   *(c)* 7·75 cm (approx.)
5. *(a)* Diagram as question 3.
    (b) Virtual / Magnified / Erect.

Spectroscopy and the Electromagnetic Spectrum

1. *(a)* Speed   *(b)* Slows down
2. *(a)* Longer   *(b)* Shorter
    (c) Shorter   *(d)* Longer
3. Line spectrum only has certain wavelengths. Continuous spectrum has all the (visible) wavelengths, e.g. solar spectrum.
4. *(a)*

Red light

    (b) $4 \cdot 76 \times 10^{14}$ Hz   *(c)* $4 \cdot 76 \times 10^{14}$ Hz

ANSWERS

5. (a) Electrons jumping from one shell to another closer to the nucleus and releasing energy (light).
   (b) No.
6. The line spectrum of an element identifies that element like a fingerprint identifies a person.
7. If the line spectrum of an element is contained within the line spectrum from the star, then the element must be present.
8. (a) No   (b) Yes   (c) Yes
9. Aerial
   Microwave probe
   Thermal imaging camera
   Eye
   Fluorescent ink
   X-ray film (photographic film)
   Photographic film.
10. (a) Gamma rays.
    (b) TV and radio waves.
    (c) Gamma rays
        X-rays
        Ultraviolet
        Visible light
        Infrared
        Microwave
        TV and Radio Waves

SECTION 2 — SPACE TRAVEL

Rockets

1. 6 m/s   2. 3 m/s
3. 2 m/s   4. 3 m/s
5. 1 m/s
6. (a) 500 N   (b) 300 N (up)
   (c) 6 m/s^2
7. (a) 12 000 N   (b) 3000 N (up)
   (c) 2·5 m/s^2
8. (a) 10 000 N (up)   (b) 5 m/s^2
9. (a) 800 kg   (b) 12·5 m/s^2
10. (a) 15 m/s^2 (b) Mass decreases
    (c) Acceleration increases.

Gravity and Weightlessness

1. The acceleration of gravity is the same for all objects (if air resistance is negligible).
2. (a) 500 N   (b) 80 N
3.

Weight / N
800
304
2112
920

4. (a) More than 600 N.
   (b) 600 N
   (c) Less than 600 N.
5. Weight on the Earth = 900 N.
   Weight 10 miles up is **less**.

Projectile motion

1. (a) 20 m/s   (b) 10 m/s
   (c) 20 m
2. (a) 50 m/s   (b) 25 m/s
   (c) 125 m
3. (a) 25 m/s   (b) 12·5 m/s
   (c) 31·25 m
4. 1. Multiply time by 10 → final velocity.
   2. Final velocity ÷ 2 → average velocity.
   3. Average velocity × time → depth of well.
5. 16·2 m
6. (a) 20 m/s   (b) 10 m
7. (a) 12 m   (b) 24 m
   (c) 42 m   (d) 51 m
   (e) 6·6 m
8. (a) 800 m   (b) 80 m
9. (a) 33·3 m/s   (b) 45 m
10. (a) Very fast projectile always falling towards the Earth but never reaches it.
    (b) Satellites orbit the Earth because they are "falling" under the force of gravity.

Re-entry

1. (a) True   (b) Yes
2. To protect the shuttle and the astronauts inside from the extreme heat.
3. Kinetic energy is converted to heat energy.
4. 75 000 kg (no change).
5. (a) High   (b) Low

NOTES

NOTES

NOTES

NOTES